QUESTIONS
&ANSWERS
from the
BIBLE

*Hundreds of
thought-provoking
questions and answers
from the Bible*

BARBOUR
PUBLISHING, INC.
Uhrichsville, Ohio

ISBN 1-55748-959-9

Published by: Barbour Publishing, Inc.
                  P.O. Box 719
                  Uhrichsville, OH 44683
                  http://www.barbourbooks.com

Printed in the United States of America.

SECTION 1

1. Who said, "Is not this great Babylon, that I have built"?
2. Finish Christ's sentence, "These ought ye to have done and not—."
3. Who said, "Days should speak, and multitude of years should teach wisdom"?
4. Who promised his people, "The Lord shall fight for you, and ye shall hold your peace"?
5. What is the verse of the Psalm that ends, "all ye lands"?
6. Who said, "Thou shalt have joy and gladness; and many shall rejoice at his birth"? To whom was it said, and of whom?
7. In what Book is the saying about the Lamb's book of life?
8. Who advised the Sanhedrin to let the Christians alone, saying that if their work was of God, it could not be overthrown?
9. Who said, "Therefore shall a man leave his father and his mother, and shall cleave unto his wife"?
10. What is Christ's saying which begins, "If the Son therefore shall make you free—"?
11. Who commanded, "Breach for breach, eye for eye, tooth for tooth"?
12. What did James say no man could tame?
13. Finish Paul's sentence, "The goodness of God leadeth—."
14. What is the rest of Christ's saying, "This kind can

come forth by nothing, but—"?

15. Who wrote, "Looking for that blessed hope, and the glorious appearing of the great God and our Saviour Jesus Christ"?

16. Who praised the man that "sweareth to his own hurt, and changeth not"?

17. Who exhorted his people, "Be not ye afraid of them: remember the LORD, which is great and terrible, and fight for your brethren, your sons, and your daughters, your wives, and your houses"?

18. In what Book is the saying, "Many waters cannot quench love"?

19. Who said, "This is my beloved Son, in whom I am well pleased"? On what occasion?

20. Who speaks about "Redeeming the time, because the days are evil"?

21. Who said, "The isles shall wait for his law"?

22. What proverb ends with "how good it is!"?

23. Finish the sentence, "Eye hath not seen, nor ear heard, neither have entered into the heart of man—."

24. Who said that in the judgment day a man shall give account of every idle word he has spoken?

25. Complete Paul's saying, "This is the will of God, even—."

SECTION 2

1. What is the rest of the proverb, "My son, if sinners entice thee—"?

2. Whose is the saying about the axe laid to the root of the trees?

3. Who said of the religious leaders that they said "Peace, peace," when there was no peace?

4. What did Paul call "the first commandment with promise"?
5. Who asked God to put his tears into his bottle?
6. Who laid his sin to "the woman whom thou gavest to be with me"?
7. Who said of God that He is "of purer eyes than to behold evil," and that He cannot look on iniquity?
8. Of whom did Christ say that they loved "the uppermost seats in the synagogues"?
9. What is the proverb about spreading a net in the sight of a bird?
10. To whom did God say, "The LORD searcheth all hearts"?
11. Who said, "Behold the handmaid of the Lord; be it unto me according to thy word"?
12. Finish Paul's saying, "The natural man receiveth not—"?
13. What is the first part of the sentence which ends, "and into his courts with praise"?
14. Of whom was it asked in astonishment whether he also was among the prophets?
15. Of whom did the Lord ask, "Who is this that darkeneth counsel by words without knowledge?"
16. Finish the quotation from Isaiah: "I will say to the north, Give up; and to the south, Keep not back."
17. What is Christ's question about spoiled salt?
18. Finish the quotation, "In that he himself hath suffered being tempted—."
19. What is the rest of the verse in Deuteronomy beginning, "If from thence thou shalt seek the Lord thy God—"?
20. What saying of Christ's concerning his preexistence

introduces Abraham?

21. What is Paul's saying about "respect of persons"?
22. What is the proverb about pride and a fall?
23. Finish the promise in Leviticus, "Ye shall lie down—."
24. In what Book is the prayer, "Lead me to the rock that is higher than I"?
25. Who said to a mighty king, "Let thy gifts be to thyself, and give thy rewards to another"?

SECTION 3

1. To whom did the Lord say, "Speak unto the children of Israel, that they go forward"?
2. In whose song are the words, "He hath put down the mighty from their seats, and exalted them of low degree"?
3. What is Paul's saying contrasting the letter and the spirit?
4. Finish Peter's saying, "One day is with the Lord as a thousand years—."
5. What is the rest of the saying, "Better is it that thou shouldest not vow—."
6. In what Book is the great affirmation, "Hear, O Israel: The LORD our God is one LORD"?
7. Who asked the question, "Shall we receive good at the hand of God, and shall we not receive evil"?
8. What proverb about grapes did Ezekiel refute?
9. Who did Christ say are His brother, his sister, and His mother?
10. Finish Paul's sentence, "Ye are all the children of God—."

11. Give the sentence from the Revelation which ends, "and their works do follow them."

12. To what does the proverb compare pleasant words?

13. Finish the words of the psalm, "My soul, wait thou only upon God; for—."

14. To whom was it said, "Dust thou art, and unto dust shalt thou return"?

15. Complete the warcry, "The sword of the LORD—."

16. Who said, "We will give ourselves continually to prayer, and to the ministry of the word"?

17. Who said of marriage, "What therefore God hath joined together, let not man put asunder"?

18. Finish the verse of the psalm, "O thou that hearest prayer—."

19. Who said, "I am doing a great work, so that I cannot come down"?

20. Finish the proverb, "Trust in the Lord with all thy heart; and—."

21. To what did Paul compare the coming of "the day of the Lord"?

22. Of whom is it said in Hebrews that of them "the world was not worthy"?

23. What is the saying in Hosea about being "joined to idols"?

24. What command follows "Cease to do evil"? Who said it?

25. What is Christ's saying about the coming night?

SECTION 4

1. What is the rest of Paul's question, "Thou therefore which teachest another—"?

2. Who said, "If I perish, I perish"?

3. What proverb begins, "In all thy ways acknowledge him—"?

4. Who said, "Know ye not that there is a prince and a great man fallen this day in Israel?" Of whom was he speaking?

5. What is Christ's saying about confessing Him before men?

6. Finish the verse of the psalm, "Thou crownest the year with thy goodness."

7. Who sung, "Who is like unto thee, O LORD, among the gods? Who is like thee, glorious in holiness, fearful in praises, doing wonders"? On what occasion?

8. Finish this sentence from Habakkuk: "Woe to him that buildeth a town with blood—."

9. After opening the eyes of man blind from birth, what did Christ say about Himself?

10. Complete the command, "Exhort one another daily—."

11. Who wrote, "The fruit of righteousness is sown in peace of them that make peace"?

12. Through whom did God promise Israel, "I have blotted out, as a thick cloud thy transgressions, and, as a cloud, thy sins?

13. Finish the sentence of the Psalm, "The LORD is merciful and gracious—."

14. Who said, "I dwell among mine own people"?

15. Who said, "I have planted, Apollos watered; but God gave the increase"?

16. Who said of death, "There the wicked cease from troubling; and there the weary be at rest"?

17. Who said, "This is my beloved Son, in whom I am

well pleased"? Of whom did He speak? When?

18. Finish Paul's words, "It is good to be zealously affected—."

19. Who said of Moses that he was "learned in all the wisdom of the Egyptians, and was mighty in words and in deeds"?

20. Complete the proverb, "The hoary head is a crown of glory, if ."

21. Who wrote, "The harvest is past, the summer is ended, and we are not saved"?

22. What two masters did Christ say we cannot serve?

23. In what Book is Christ reported as calling himself "Alpha and Omega, the first and the last"?

24. Whose are the words, "Thou art weighed in the balances, and art found wanting"? To what king were they addressed?

25. "As far as the east is from the west—"; finish the sentence.

SECTION 5

1. Finish the sentence, "Ye have not yet resisted unto blood—."

2. Who said, "The most High dwelleth not in temples made with hands"?

3. Who asked, "Am I my brother's keeper"?

4. Of whom was it said, when he died at the age of one hundred and twenty, "His eye was not dim, nor his natural force abated"?

5. Complete the prayer, "Create in me a clean heart, O God—."

6. Finish Christ's saying, "Suffer the little children—."

7. Who said, "I am he that liveth, and was dead; and, behold, I am alive for evermore"?

8. Finish the proverb, "Whom the Lord loveth—."

9. Who said, "The half was not told me," and concerning whom?

10. Fill out the verse, "In thy presence—," "at thy right hand."

11. Complete Christ's questions, "Is not the life more than meat—."

12. Who said, "Let God be true, but every man a liar"?

13. Who asked, "Is there no balm in Gilead; is there no physician there?"

14. Who spoke of the time "when the morning stars sang together, and all the sons of God shouted for joy"?

15. Who asked, "Should such a man as I flee?"

16. Who said, "One thing I know, that, whereas I was blind, now I see"?

17. What is the first part of the sentence ending "loadeth us with benefits"?

18. Who said, "My punishment is greater than I can bear"?

19. Who wrote, "There is one God, and one mediator between God and men, the man Christ Jesus"?

20. Who said, "Follow me, and I will make you fishers of men"? To whom?

21. Who wrote, "Then shall we know, if we follow on to know the Lord"?

22. Complete Christ's saying, "A man's life consisteth not—."

23. Who wrote, "The soul that sinneth, it shall die"?

24. Who received this commandment regarding the law of God: "Turn not from it to the right hand or to the

left, that thou mayest prosper withersoever thou goest"?

25. Complete this quotation from Habakkuk: "The earth shall be filled with the knowledge of the glory of the LORD—."

SECTION 6

1. What verse of a psalm about zeal was quoted with reference to Christ?
2. What verse in Hosea contrasts mercy and sacrifice?
3. What is the verse about God's love and his chastening?
4. What is the great saying about Enoch?
5. Who said, "Woe unto him that striveth with his Maker!"
6. Finish the proverb that says of wisdom, "Length of days is in her right hand—."
7. Who asked Christ the question, "Good Master, what shall I do that I may inherit eternal life?"
8. Complete Paul's sentence, "Where the spirit of the Lord is—."
9. What Book tells about "the song of Moses and the Lamb"?
10. What is the rest of the prayer of David beginning, "O LORD, open thou my lips—"?
11. Whose song begins, "Sing ye to the LORD, for he hath triumphed gloriously"?
12. Who received the promise that, if he meditated on God's law, "Then thou shalt make thy way prosperous, and then thou shalt have good success"?
13. Who express the wish, "Oh that my head were waters,

and mine eyes a fountain of tears!"

14. What prophet cried, "Woe unto him that giveth his neighbor drink"?

15. Finish the beatitude, "Blessed are the poor in spirit—."

16. What is Paul's saying about "the yoke of bondage"?

17. Of what occasion is it said, "So they read in the book in the law of God distinctly, and gave the sense, and caused them to understand the reading"?

18. Of whose pursuit of the enemy is the phrase used, "Faint, yet pursuing"?

19. What verse of a psalm speaks of God's pity of his children?

20. In what parable is the expression, "Take thine ease, eat, drink, and be merry"?

21. Finish Paul's saying, "In Jesus Christ neither circumcision availeth anything, nor uncircumcision; but—."

22. Complete the saying in Job, "They that plow iniquity, and sow wickedness—."

23. What prophet commanded, "Make you a new heart and a new spirit; for why will ye die"?

24. What is Christ's saying about climbing up "some other way" into the sheepfold?

25. What is the proverb about wisdom being "the principal thing"?

SECTION 7

1. What is Christ's saying about the lilies of the field?

2. Finish Peter's sentence, "The Lord is not slack concerning his promise, as some men count slackness—."

3. What Bible heroine did King Ahaserus promise half

of his kingdom?

4. Finish the command in Deuteronomy: "Thou shalt love the LORD thy God with—."

5. What is the first part of the proverb which ends, "and a brother is born for adversity"?

6. Finish Hosea's sentence, "They have sown the wind—."

7. What is Paul's saying concerning the Christian's breastplate and helmet?

8. What is Isaiah's saying about sins being as snow and as wool?

9. Who sung, "He hath filled the hungry with good things; and the rich he hath sent empty away"?

10. Who said, "There is none righteous, no, not one."

11. Finish the sentence, "Be not drunk with wine, wherein is excess; but—."

12. What is the psalm prayer that speaks of the apple of the eye?

13. Who was bidden to fight when he heard "the sound of a going in the tops of the mulberry trees"?

14. Who said to the sea, "Hitherto shalt thou come, but no further: and here shall thy proud waves be stayed"?

15. Whose decree was "according to the law of the Medes and Persians, which altereth not"?

16. Finish Paul's sentence, "We are labourers together with God."

17. Complete the Beatitude, "Blessed are they that mourn—."

18. Of whom did the children of Belial say, "How shall this man save us"?

19. Who said, "My spirit shall not always strive with

man," and when?

20. Who asked the question, "is it well with the child?"
21. In what Book is it said, "The king himself is served by the field"?
22. Who said, "Who hath ears to hear, let him hear"?
23. What is Paul's description of the house of God?
24. Who said, "All things come of thee, and of thine own have we given thee"?
25. Finish the saying, "We are made partakers of Christ, if—."

SECTION 8

1. Finish the sentence in Hebrews beginning, "No chastening for the present seemeth to be joyous, but grievous—."
2. What king said to his subjects, "My little finger shall be thicker than my father's loins"?
3. Who said, "Ye ask, and receive not, because ye ask amiss"?
4. Who said, on starting on a journey, "Rise up, Lord, and let thine enemies be scattered"?
5. To what church did the Spirit send the message, "Thou hast left thy first love"?
6. To whom did the Lord give the promise, "Five of you shall chase an hundred, and an hundred of you shall put ten thousand to flight"?
7. What description of the path of the just is in the Book of Proverbs?
8. Finish Isaiah's sentence, "Look unto me, and be ye saved—."
9. What is the blessing of the meek?

10. Finish Paul's sentence, "All have sinned—."
11. What is the proverb about a merry heart?
12. Who said of the power of Israel, "I will overturn, overturn, overturn it: and it shall be no more, until he come whose right it is, and I will give it him"?
13. Who asked, "What shall be done unto the man whom the king delighteth to honor?"
14. Finish the sentence, "God, who commanded the light to shine out of darkness, hath shined in our hearts—."
15. Of whom was it said at his birth, "What manner of child shall this be?"
16. Who prophesied, "They shall beat their swords into plowshares and their spears into pruning hooks"?
17. Who said, "The joy of the LORD is your strength"?
18. Of whom was it said that he was "very meek, above all the men who were upon the face of the earth"?
19. Who was asked, "Canst thou bind the sweet influences of Pleiades, or loose the bands of Orion?"
20. Finish Christ's sentence, "Seek ye first the kingdom of God, and his righteousness—."
21. In what Book is the saying about Armageddon?
22. Who said of Christ that He "died for us, that, whether we wake or sleep, we should live together with him"?
23. Finish the verse of the psalm beginning, "The sacrifices of God are—."
24. Of what did Moses speak when he said, "This is the bread which the LORD hath given you to eat"?
25. Who said, "The dayspring from on high hath visited us"?

SECTION 9

1. Finish Christ's saying, "Whosoever hath, to him shall be given, and he shall have more abundance: but—."

2. Complete Christ's saying, "I am the door: by me if any man enter in—."

3. What is the rest of the verse in the psalm beginning, "The mountains shall bring peace to the people—"?

4. Of what time was it said, "There were giants in the earth in those days"?

5. In what Book are the words, "To day if ye will hear his voice, harden not your hearts"?

6. Who said, "I see the heavens opened, and the Son of man standing on the right hand of God"?

7. To whom did Christ say, "Lackest thou one thing"?

8. What prophet said, "Ye have plowed wickedness, ye have reaped iniquity"?

9. What does Ecclesiastes say about him "that loveth silver"?

10. What verse of the psalms contains seven names for the Lord?

11. Who asked God, "Give me now wisdom and knowledge, that I may go out and come in before this people"?

12. What is Christ's promise for those "which do hunger and thirst after righeousness"?

13. What is Paul's "foundation saying"?

14. What is the proverb about keeping the heart?

15. Who asked in dismay, "How shall the ark of the Lord come to me"?

16. What saying about God's laws was the origin of the phylacteries?

17. Who said, "it is not in man that walketh to direct his steps"?
18. What are Paul's directions for the training of children?
19. To what church did Jesus say, "Be thou faithful unto death, and I will give thee a crown of life"?
20. In what words did God exhort Joshua to courage?
21. Who said, "My God hath sent his angel, and hath shut the lions' mouths"?
22. Who said, "Your Father knoweth that ye have need of these things"?
23. Who said, "Great is the mystery of godliness"?
24. What was Peter's prophecy of "new heavens and a new earth"?
25. What simile does the psalmist use to express the brevity of human life?

SECTION 10

1. To what prophet was it said, "O thou man of God, there is death in the pot"?
2. Finish this quotation from Job: "Shall mortal man be more just than God?"
3. Complete this sentence Habakkuk: "The Lord is in his holy temple—."
4. What is the Beatitude for the merciful?
5. What is Paul's saying about the leaven?
6. What is James's saying about humility?
7. What is the proverb that urges independence?
8. What is the beginning of the verse of the psalm which ends, "he drew me out of many waters"?
9. What king said to his subjects, "My father hath

chastised you with whips, but I will chastise you with scorpions"?

10. Who said, "Blessed are your eyes, for they see: and your ears, for they hear"?

11. Who wrote, "See that none render evil for evil unto any man; but ever follow that which is good"?

12. Who said, "There shall not be a man put to death this day: for today the LORD hath wrought salvation in Israel"?

13. Finish the quotation, "Lift up the hands which hang down."

14. Who said, "Whatsoever cometh forth of the doors of my house to meet me, when I return in peace from the children of Ammon, shall surely be the LORD's, and I will offer it up for a burnt offering"?

15. What was God's promise to the aged in the Book of Isaiah?

16. Who cried in death, "Lord Jesus, receive my spirit"?

17. In what parable are the words, "Yet hath he not root in himself"?

18. Finish the proverb, "Even a fool, when he holdeth his peace—."

19. Who said, "While the earth remaineth, seed time and harvest, and cold and heat, and summer and winter, and day and night shall not cease"? When was it said?

20. Who asked of his people, "Whose ox have I taken? Or whose ass have I taken? or whom have I defrauded? whom have I oppressed? or of whose hand have I received any bribe?"

21. In what Book is the song, "Alleluia: for the Lord God omnipotent reigneth"?

22. Who said of Christ that He "was delivered for our

offences, and was raised again for our justification"?

23. Finish this verse of the psalm, "The mercy of the Lord is from everlasting to everlasting—."

24. Of what substance is it said, "He that gathered much had nothing over, and he that gathered little had no lack"?

25. Complete the quotation, "There is a spirit in man: and —."

SECTION 11

1. Finish this sentence from Hosea: "I drew them with cords of a man—."

2. Complete Christ's saying: "I am the good shepherd—."

3. What Book contains the saying about the white stone and the new name?

4. Who said to his priests, "Ye shall stand still in Jordan"?

5. Finish this verse from the psalm: "The LORD hath prepared his throne in the heavens—."

6. What is Christ's saying about taking thought for the morrow?

7. What is Paul's saying about "every creature of God"?

8. Who said, "We saw the children of Anak there"?

9. Who said, "Thou art a God ready to pardon, gracious and merciful, slow to anger, and of great kindness"?

10. What is the Beatitude of the pure in heart?

11. What was Paul's statement of the test of one's work?

12. Of whom was it said that they "out of weakness were made strong"?

13. In what Book is it said of God's laws, "Thou shalt

write them upon the posts of thy house, and on they-gates"?

14. Who has said, "There is no God"?

15. What is the conclusion of Habakkuk's sentence, "Although the fig tree shall not blossom, neither shall fruit be in the vines; the labour of the olive shall fail, and the fields shall yield no meat; and the flock shall be cut off from the fold, and there shall be no herd in the stalls—"?

16. What is the conclusion of the parable of the rich fool?

17. What is the end of James' sentence, "Resist the devil, and—"?

18. Who was tested by his pronunciation of Shibboleth?

19. Whose was the urging, "Come ye, and let us walk in the light of the Lord"?

20. What was Christ's saying about trust in riches?

21. Who said "Rejoice evermore"?

22. Who asked "Can the Ethiopian change his skin, or the leopard his spots"?

23. Finish this sentence from Job: "Wrath killed the foolish man—."

24. Complete this saying from Ecclesiastes: "When goods increase—."

25. Who cried, as he was stoned to death, "Lord, lay not this sin to their charge"?

SECTION 12

1. Of whom is it said, "There was no room for them in the inn"?

2. Who said to God, "Behold, heaven and the heaven of heavens cannot contain thee; how much less this

house which I have built!'"?

3. To whom did God say, "Whoso sheddeth man's blood, by man shall his blood be shed"?

4. What promise is in the Psalms for "the poor of the people"?

5. What is the proverb about the ant?

6. Finish Paul's saying, "We faint not; but though our outward man perish—."

7. Who wrote, "God is light, and in him is no darkness at all"?

8. Who said, "Am I God, to kill and to make alive?"

9. To what prophet was it said, "Son of man, I take away from thee the desire of thine eyes with a stroke"?

10. What is Christ's saying about judging others?

11. Finish Paul's saying, "All the law is fulfilled in one word, even in this—."

12. Who said to God, "I have heard of thee by the hearing of the ear: but now mine eye seeth thee"?

13. Of whom was it said that the Lord blessed his house because of the ark of God?

14. What is the eyeservice verse in Ephesians?

15. What is the Beatitude for the peacemakers?

16. What verse of the psalm is about a candle?

17. Who raised the warcry, "To your tents, O Israel"?

18. Who commanded, "Pray without ceasing"?

19. In what Book is God called "the Ancient of days"?

20. Finish the sentence from Hebrews: "They could not enter in—."

21. Who said of Canaan, "Let us go up at once, and possess it; for we are well able to overcome it"?

22. Finish the verse from the psalm: "Who is God save the Lord?"

23. Finish Christ's sentence, "As the Father knoweth me—."
24. What is Paul's great verse about justification by faith?
25. In what Book are the words, "The Lord thy God in the mist of thee is mighty; he will save, he will rejoice over thee with joy; he will rest in his love, he will joy over thee with singing"?

SECTION 13

1. Of whom is it said that he "danced before the Lord with all his might"?
2. What is the Beatitude for the persecuted?
3. What is Paul's saying about our being God's temple?
4. In what Book is the prophecy, "Many of them that sleep in the dust of the earth shall awake, some to everlasting life, and some to shame and everlasting contempt?
5. Finish Christ's saying, "Fear not, little flock—."
6. In what Book is the saying, "Blessed are they which are called unto the marriage supper of the Lamb"?
7. Complete the verse from Isaiah: "The lofty looks of man shall be humbled, and the haughtiness of men shall be bowed down—."
8. Who asked, "Why is the house of God forsaken?"
9. What is Christ's saying about the needle's eye?
10. Of whom was it falsely said, "This man is the great power of God"?
11. What is the proverb about the sleep of the sluggard?
12. Who said, "Now I know that the Lord is greater than all gods," and when did he say it?
13. Finish the saying in Job, "Man is born unto trouble,

as—."

14. Complete Paul's sentence, "With good will doing service—."

15. What is Christ's saying about His "other sheep"?

16. Finish Jeremiah's sentence, "Cursed be the man that trusteth in man, and maketh flesh his arm—."

17. What is the rainbow verse of Genesis?

18. What is Paul's saying about walking in the Spirit?

19. What did John say about the result of walking in the light?

20. What did Paul say about earthen vessels?

21. Complete the sentence, "The heavens declare the glory of God—."

22. Finish the proverb: "The name of the LORD is a strong tower—."

23. Who said, "LORD, it is nothing with thee to help, whether with many, or with them that have no power"?

24. Where is the verse, "There is no peace, saith the LORD, unto the wicked"?

25. To whom did an angel say, "I bring you good tidings of great joy, which shall be to all people"?

SECTION 14

1. What is Christ's saying about "the deceitfulness of riches"?

2. Who said, "In everything give thanks: for this is the will of God in Christ Jesus concerning you"?

3. To what prophet did God say, if he prophesied faithfully, "Thou hast delivered thy soul"?

4. What is the verse of the psalm about rain on the

mown grass?

5. What Book did Christ quote when He answered Satan, "Ye shall not tempt the Lord your God"?

6. What is Christ's saying about the mote and the beam?

7. What is Paul's saying about bodily exercise?

8. Who said, "My father, if the prophet had bid thee do some great thing, wouldest thou not have done it?"

9. What does Ecclesiastes say about a workingman's sleep?

10. To whom did the Lord say, "I bare you on eagles' wings, and brought you unto myself"?

11. What is the origin of the saying, "What mean these stones?"

12. To what church did the spirit say, "Thou hast a name that thou livest, and art dead"?

13. In what Book is the sentence, "The trees of the Lord are full of sap"?

14. Who proposed the riddle, "Out of the eater came forth meat, and out of the strong came forth sweetness"?

15. Finish the verse of the psalm, "He shall have dominion also from sea to sea—."

16. Who called the disciples "the salt of the earth"?

17. Finish the verse in Hebrews, "There remaineth therefore a rest—."

18. Who received from God the command, "Thou shalt drink of the brook, and I have commanded the ravens to feed thee there"?

19. In what Book is the command, "Follow peace with all men, and holiness, without which no man shall see the Lord"?

20. Complete the saying of the psalm: "O Lord, how manifold are thy works!"

21. What is Christ's saying about our treasure?
22. What is the conclusion of James' sentence, "Draw nigh to God—"?
23. Who said of the temple, "Is it time for you, O ye, to dwell in your ceiled houses, and this house lie waste?"
24. What is the other half of the couplet, "I will sing unto the Lord as long as I live"?
25. Who said, "Blessed is the man that trusteth in the Lord, and whose hope the Lord is"?

SECTION 15

1. What is Paul's saying about "our light affliction"?
2. What is Christ's command urging us to be ready for His coming?
3. Who wrote, "Cease ye from man, whose breath is in his nostrils"?
4. Who said, "What evil thing is this that ye do, and profane the sabbath day?"
5. Who said, "Be strong in the Lord, and in the power of his might"?
6. Who said, "With God all things are possible"?
7. Of whom was it said that he was "a mighty hunter before the Lord"?
8. Complete the couplet beginning, "The law of the Lord is perfect, converting the soul."
9. To whom did the Lord say, "I have no pleasure in the death of the wicked"?
10. Whose is the command, "Quench not the Spirit"?
11. Finish Christ's saying, "Let your light so shine before men—."
12. What prophet said to Asa, "The Lord is with you,

while ye be with him; and if ye seek him, he will be found of you; but if ye forsake him, he will forsake you"?

13. To whom did God say, "Ye shall be unto me a kingdom of priests, and an holy nation"?

14. What Book speaks of "the general assembly and church of the firstborn, which are written in heaven"?

15. To whom did Peter say, "Thy money perish with thee, because thou hast thought that the gift of God may be purchased with money"?

16. Who said, "There shall be one fold, and one shepherd"?

17. Finish the proverb beginning, "My son, keep thy father's commandment—."

18. Complete this verse from Job: "Happy is the man whom God correcteth: therefore—."

19. What is the rest of James' sentence, "Humble yourselves in the sight of the Lord, and —."

20. Who said, "Unto you is born this day in the city of David a Saviour, which is Christ the Lord"? To whom was it said?

21. Who uttered the prophecy, "I will also give thee for a light to the Gentiles, that thou mayest be my salvation unto the end of the earth"?

22. What prophet said, "I will ransom them from the power of the grave; I will redeem them from death: O death, I will be thy plagues; O grave, I will be thy destruction"?

23. Who wrote: "Tribulation worketh patience; and patience, experience; and experience, hope"?

24. Who warned against weeding the tares out from the wheat?

25. What Book says, "All the labour of man is for his mouth, and yet the appetite is not filled"?

SECTION 16

1. What did Christ say about His power over His own life?
2. To whom did the Israelites say, "All that the LORD hath spoken we will do"?
3. Complete the psalm couplet: "He shall deliver the needy when he crieth—."
4. What did Paul say about "the wisdom of this world"?
5. Finish John's sentence, "If we say that we have no sin—."
6. "Before honour," says the proverb, is—what?
7. Where was it said, "Go to, let us build us a city and a tower, whose top may reach unto heaven"?
8. What prophet, describing women's attire, predicts for them "burning instead of beauty"?
9. What saying of Christ introduces dogs and pigs?
10. Whom did Paul advise, "Let no man despise thy youth"?
11. To what church did Christ send the message, "Thou hast a little strength, and hast kept my word, and hast not denied my name"?
12. Finish the verse of the psalm: "Men shall be blessed in him—."
13. Where in the Bible is the reference to "the house of bondage"?
14. What is the prophecy in Daniel for those "that be wise"?
15. Who said, "Many that are first shall be last; and the

27

last first"?

16. Complete Paul's saying "When we were yet without strength—."

17. Give the verse in Hebrews comparing the word of God to a sword.

18. Finish the verse, "Blessed are the undefiled in the way—."

19. Who said, "When I bow down myself in the house of Rimmon, the LORD pardon thy servant in this thing"?

20. What is the saying about the bag with holes?

21. Who said, "Unto whomsoever much is given, of him shall be much required"?

22. What is Paul's saying about the conflict between the flesh and the Spirit?

23. To whom did Elijah say, "The barrel of meal shall not waste, neither shall the cruse of oil fail, until the day that the LORD sendeth rain upon the earth"?

24. Who said, "Rebel not ye against the Lord, neither fear ye the people of the land; for they are bread for us"?

25. Who said of Christ, "He hath on his vesture and on his thigh a name written, KING OF KINGS, AND LORD OF LORDS"?

SECTION 17

1. Who said to the Israelites, "Thou shalt remember all the way which the Lord thy God led thee these forty years in the wilderness, to humble thee, and to prove thee"?

2. Who sung, "Glory to God in the highest, and on earth

peace, good will toward men"? Where?

3. Who wrote, "God commandeth his love toward us, in that, while we were yet sinners, Christ died for us"?

4. Who upbraided David for his dancing before the LORD?

5. What is the proverb about the power of the tongue?

6. What is Christ's saying about asking, seeking, and knocking?

7. Who said, "If ye had not plowed with my heifer, ye had not found out my riddle"?

8. What is the psalmist's answer to the question, "Wherewithal shall a young man cleanse his way"?

9. What is the comparison of life to mist?

10. Who said, "As captain of the host of the LORD am I now come"?

11. Who prophesied, "They shall not hunger nor thirst; neither shall the heat nor sun smite them: for he that hath mercy on them shall lead them, even by the springs of water shall he guide them"?

12. Who said, "I have a baptism to be baptized with; and how am I straitened till it be accomplished!"?

13. What is the conclusion of Paul's exhortation, "Prove all things"?

14. What is the first Commandment?

15. What is the shuttle verse of Job?

16. What is the honeycomb comparison to God's judgments?

17. Whom did Christ ask, "Can ye drink of the cup that I drink of? and be baptized with the baptism that I am baptized with"?

18. What is Paul's saying urging thought about the unseen world?

19. What is the verse in Revelation about the new heaven and new earth?
20. What is the saying that begins, "Take with you words, and turn to the LORD—"?
21. Finish the sentence, "Thou shalt guide me with thy counsel—."
22. Complete Isaiah's sentence, "And he looked for judgment, but behold oppression—."
23. What is the conclusion of Christ's saying, "If ye then, being evil, know how to give good gifts unto your children—"?
24. Complete Paul's sentence, "Whether Paul, or Apollos, or Cephas, or the world, or life, or death, or things present, or things to come, —."
25. Who said, "I perceive that thou art in the gall of bitterness, and in the bond of iniquity"? To whom was he speaking?

SECTION 18

1. What is the saying in Ecclesiastes about the house of mourning?
2. To whom did God say, "I will bless thee. . .and thou shalt be a blessing"?
3. What did Christ say about His sheep?
4. Whom did Paul urge, "Neglect not the gift that is in thee"?
5. Finish the sentence, "Thy word have I hid in mine heart—."
6. What is the second Commandment?
7. In what Book are the words, "Thou shalt remember the Lord thy God: for it is he that giveth thee power

to get wealth"?

8. Finish the proverb, "Can a man take fire in his bosom—."

9. What parable ends with the words, "Then shall the righteous shine forth as the sun in the kingdom of their Father"?

10. Complete Paul's saying, "As by one man's disobedience many were made sinners—."

11. Finish James's sentence, "To him that knoweth to do good, and doeth it not—."

12. Who said, "Lord, now lettest thou thy servant depart in peace?" On what occasion?

13. What is Jeremiah's saying about the deceitful heart?

14. Who said, "Hear now, ye rebels; must we fetch you water out of this rock?" Where?

15. What is the chief proverb about friendship?

16. What did Christ say about fulfilment of Scripture?

17. What is "the fruit of the Spirit?"

18. What is the prophecy of "the desire of all nations"?

19. What is Paul's list of the gospel armor?

20. What is Ezekiel's saying about the stony heart?

21. Who said, "I would not live alway"?

22. Complete the verse of the psalm, "He satisfieth the longing soul—."

23. Who said, "With the jawbone of an ass, heaps upon heaps, with the jawbone of an ass have I slain a thousand men"?

24. Where is it said of Christ that He was "in all points tempted like as we are, yet without sin"?

25. To what church did Christ say, "Because thou art lukewarm, and neither cold nor hot, I will spue thee out of my mouth"?

SECTION 19

1. What is the first verse of John's Gospel?
2. What prophet speaks about "making the ephah small, and the shekel great, and falsifying the balances by deceit"?
3. Who said, "Art thou he that troubleth Israel?" To whom did he say it?
4. Finish this sentence from 1 John: "If we confess our sins—."
5. What prophet said, "The eyes of the LORD run to and fro throughout the whole earth, to shew himself strong in the behalf of them whose heart is perfect toward him"?
6. Who said, "Shout; for the LORD hath given you the city"? To what city did he refer?
7. What Book say, "Our God is a consuming fire"?
8. Who said, "My kingdom is not of this world"?
9. Who said, "The leprosy therefore of Naaman shall cleave unto thee, and unto thy seed forever"? To whom was he speaking?
10. Who said, "Behold, this dreamer cometh"? To whom did they refer?
11. Repeat the prayer beginning, "Let the words of my mouth—."
12. Who said, "Except ye repent, ye shall all likewise perish"?
13. Who said, "To me to live is Christ, and to die is gain"?
14. In what Book is the promise regarding the hereafter, "God shall wipe away all tears from their eyes"?
15. Who asked, "How should a man be just with God?"

16. What is the third Commandment?
17. Who said, "I set before you this day a blessing and a curse"?
18. Who said, "Woe unto them that are wise in their own eyes, and prudent in their own sight!"?
19. What is Christ's saying about the right eye offending?
20. What is Paul's saying about being dead to sin?
21. What proverb tells us what to do with God's commandments?
22. Finish the verse, "My flesh and my heart faileth: but—."
23. Complete Christ's saying, "The Son of man came not be to ministered unto—."
24. In whose prophecy in God's promise, "I will heal their backsliding, I will love them freely"?
25. Finish the prayer of the psalm: "Open thou mine eyes, that—."

SECTION 20

1. Who said, "Swear not at all"?
2. Who said, "If any provide not for his own, and specially for those of his own house, he hath denied the faith, and is worse than an infidel"?
3. Of whom was it said, "A sword shall pierce through thy own soul also"? Who said it?
4. Who wrote, "In the name of our God we will set up our banners"?
5. Who said generously, "Is not the whole land before thee?" To whom did he say it?
6. Of whom did Jehoshaphat say, "I hate him; for he

never prophesied good unto me, but always evil"?

7. Who wrote, "Heal me, O LORD, and I shall be healed; save me, and I shall be saved"?

8. What did Christ say was the reason for His coming into the world?

9. Complete Paul's prophecy: "We know that if our earthly house of this tabernacle were dissolved—."

10. Of whose vision was it said, "Every thing. . .whithersoever the river cometh shall live"?

11. What is the fourth Commandment?

12. Finish the proverb, "He that hath pity upon the poor—."

13. Who compared the kingdom of heaven to a "pearl of great price"?

14. What is Paul's statement about the requirement of a steward?

15. What is Christ's saying about the narrow gate?

16. To what does Ecclesiastes compare the laughter of fools?

17. What prophet predicted a famine, "not a famine of bread, nor a thirst for water, but of hearing the words of the LORD"?

18. What Book tells of those "that go down to the sea in ships, that do business in great waters"?

19. Who were made "hewers of wood and drawers of water," and why?

20. Who said, "The LORD God hath given me the tongue of the learned, that I should know how to speak a word in season to him that is weary"?

21. What is Christ's affirmation of union with God?

22. What is the promise in the Revelation to him "that overcometh"?

23. What is the psalmist's expression of delight in God's law?
24. Who said, "Let me die with the Philistines"?
25. Who said, "Understandest thou what thou readest?" and to whom was he speaking?

SECTION 21

1. Who said, "Fear not: for they that be with us are more than they that be with them"? On what occasion?
2. Who said, "The silver is mine, and the gold is mine, saith the Lord of hosts"?
3. Who called Herod "That fox"?
4. What are Paul's two commands about burden-bearing?
5. What is the Golden Rule?
6. In what Book are the questions, "Canst thou by searching find out God? canst thou find out the Almighty unto perfection?"
7. Who asked, "How long halt ye between two opinions? if the Lord be God, follow him: but if Baal, then follow him"?
8. Who said, "Our soul loatheth this light bread"?
9. Who commanded, "Abstain from all appearance of evil"?
10. Where in the Bible is the benediction beginning, "The Lord hear thee in the day of trouble"?
11. Finish the sentence, "Let us therefore come boldly unto the throne of grace—."
12. Who said, "How can I do this great wickedness, and sin against God?" To whom was he speaking?

13. What is the fifth Commandment?
14. Who said, "Behold, we count them happy which endure"?
15. Where did Christ say, "A prophet is not without honour, save in his own country, and in his own house"?
16. What prophet wrote: "Though thou exalt thyself as the eagle, and though thou set thy nest among the stars, thence will I bring thee down, saith the Lord"?
17. What verse of the psalms compares the Bible to a lamp?
18. Complete this verse of Isaiah: "Therefore the redeemed of the LORD shall return, and come with singing unto Zion; and everlasting joy shall be upon their head—."
19. In what Book is the prophecy: "The LORD thy God will raise up unto thee a prophet from the midst of thee, of thy brethren, like unto me; unto him ye shall harken"?
20. What king said to his judges, "Deal courageously, and the Lord shall be with the good"?
21. What is the proverb comparing wisdom to rubies?
22. Who said, "Behold the man!" Of whom did he say it?
23. Who said, "It is hard for thee to kick against the pricks"? To whom?
24. Finish the verse, "Thy way, O God, is in the sanctuary—."
25. What prophet said, "Cursed be the day wherein I was born"?

SECTION 22

1. Through what prophet did God say, "I am like a green fir tree. From me is thy fruit found"?
2. Who said, "If I do not the works of my Father, believe me not"?
3. Finish Paul's saying, "Let nothing be done through strife or vainglory—."
4. To whom did God say, "All the land which thou seest, to thee will I give it, and to thy seed forever"?
5. What does the psalmist say is "the beginning of wisdom"?
6. What prophet saw trees, "the fruit thereof shall be for meat, and the leaf thereof for medicine"?
7. What is the conclusion of Christ's saying, "Let your communication be Yea, yea; Nay, nay: for—"?
8. Who said to Christ, "Lord, what wilt thou have me to do"?
9. Complete the saying regarding Christ, "Though he were a Son, —."
10. What is Isaiah's condemnation of great land holdings?
11. Who said, "Sun, stand thou still upon Gibeon; and thou, Moon, in the valley of Ajalon"?
12. What is the sixth Commandment?
13. What psalm verse begins, "The entrance of thy words giveth light"?
14. Who cried, "Jesus, thou Son of David, have mercy on me"?
15. What saying of Paul's urges the payment of pastors' salaries?
16. What is the saying in Ecclesiastes teaching us not to

overrate the past?

17. Who said, "The LORD deal kindly with you, as ye have dealt with the dead, and with me"? To whom did she say it?

18. What verse in John describes Christ's work in creation?

19. To whom did Abraham say, "I will not take any thing that is thine, lest thou shouldest say, I have made Abram rich"?

20. Who said, "How shall I curse, whom God hath not cursed? or how shall I defy, whom the LORD hath not defied?"

21. In what prophecy are the words, "Rend you heart, and not your garments, and turn unto the Lord your God: for he is gracious and merciful, slow to anger, and of great kindness, and repenteth him of the evil"?

22. Finish Paul's saying, "If thou shalt confess with thy mouth the LORD Jesus—."

23. What is the conclusion of the verse, "I saw no temple therein—"?

24. Who said, "Do not interpretations belong to God?"

25. Who said, It is not lawful for thee to have her?"

SECTION 23

1. Who said, "Give alms of such things as ye have"?

2. Who wrote, "Walk worthy of God, who hath called you unto his kingdom and glory"?

3. In what Book are the words, "Before they call, I will answer; and while they are yet speaking, I will hear"?

4. Who named a stone Ebenezer, meaning, "Hitherto

hath the Lord helped us"?

5. Who wrote, "The fool hath said in his heart, There is no God"?
6. Who said of God, "His kingdom is an everlasting kingdom"?
7. Who said, "We cannot but speak the things which we have seen and heard"? In what Book?
8. Who wrote, "The kingdoms of this world are become the kingdoms of our Lord, and of his Christ; and he shall reign for ever and ever"? In what Book?
9. Who said, "All things are possible to him that believeth"? To whom?
10. Who said, "Let there be light," and there was light? In what Book?
11. In what Book is the benediction, "The Lord bless thee, and keep thee: the Lord make his face shine upon thee, and be gracious unto thee: the Lord lift up his countenance upon thee, and give thee peace"?
12. Who said, "He that is not with me is against me"?
13. Who wrote, "Walk in love"?
14. Who wrote, "The tongue is a fire"?
15. In what Book is the expression, "The valley of Achor for a door of hope"?
16. Who said, "I am but a little child: I know not how to go out or come in"?
17. Who said, "Choose you this day whom ye will serve"?
18. Who said "We have seen his star in the east"?
19. Who wrote, "I am not ashamed of the gospel of Christ"? In what Book?
20. In what Book is the question, "How shall we escape, if we neglect so great salvation?"

21. Who wrote, "A bruised reed shall he not break, and smoking flax shall he not quench"?
22. In what Book is this found: "Every beast of the forest is mine, and the cattle upon a thousand hills"?
23. Who said, "My father, my father, the chariot of Israel, and the horsemen thereof"? Of whom did he say it?
24. Who said, "The LORD gave, and the LORD hath taken away; blessed be the name of the LORD"?
25. To whom was it said, "I have made thee a watchman unto the house of Israel"?

SECTION 24

1. Who said, "Ye shall know the truth, and the truth shall make you free"?
2. Who wrote, "God hath chosen the weak things of the world to confound the things which are mighty"?
3. Who said, "This day shall be unto you for a memorial"? Through whom did he say it, and of what day?
4. Who said, "The fear of the LORD, that is wisdom; and to depart from evil is understanding"?
5. Who said, "Go ye into all the world, and preach the gospel to every creature"?
6. In what Book is the description of a woman, that she is "fair as the moon, clear as the sun, and terrible as an army with banners"?
7. Who wrote, "I am crucified with Christ"?
8. Who prayed, "Oh that I had wings like a dove! for then would I fly away, and be at rest"?
9. Who said, "Thou wilt cast all their sins into the depths of the sea"?

10. Who wrote, "Christ Jesus came into the world to save sinners, of whom I am chief"?

11. Who said, "How are the mighty fallen!" On what occasion?

12. In what Book is the saying, "Ye that love the Lord, hate evil"?

13. In what Book do we find: "Whatsoever God doeth, it shall be for ever"?

14. Who wrote, "All the promises of God in him [Christ] are yea, and in him Amen"?

15. In what Book is the sentence, "The eyes of the Lord are in every place, beholding the evil and the good'"?

16. Whose preaching is summed up in the words, "Repent ye: for the kingdom of heaven is at hand"?

17. Who wrote, "Unto the pure all things are pure"?

18. Who said, "Ye shall not fear them: for the Lord your God he shall fight for you"? To whom did he say it?

19. In what Book is the exhortation, "Let everything that hath breath praise the Lord"?

20. Of whom was it said that "he endured, as seeing him who is invisible"? In what Book is the saying?

21. In what Book is it commanded, "Put difference between holy and unholy, and between unclean and clean'"?

22. Who said, "Shall I drink the blood of these men, that have put their lives in jeopardy?" and on what occasion?

23. Who wrote, "No prophecy of the scripture is of any private interpretation"?

24. Of whom was it said that he "had prepared his heart to seek the law of the LORD, and to do it, and to teach in Israel statutes and judgments"?

25. Who wrote the benediction beginning, "Now unto him that is able to keep you from falling"?

SECTION 25

1. Who enacted the law "that every man should bear rule in his own house"?

2. Who said, "As thy days, so shall thy strength be"? Of whom was it said?

3. Who said, "The fear of the LORD is the beginning of knowledge?

4. Who said, "Out of the abundance of the heart the mouth speaketh"?

5. Who wrote, "Study to be quiet, and to do your own business, and to work with your own hands"? To whom was he writing?

6. Who said, "All that a man hath will he give for his life"? Of whom did he say it?

7. Who said, "Let us make man in our image, after our likeness"?

8. Who wrote, "Make a joyful noise unto the LORD, all the earth"?

9. Who said, "Ah, LORD God! Behold, I cannot speak: for I am a child"? On what occasion?

10. Who said, "Lord, I believe; help thou mine unbelief"? To whom did he say it?

11. In what Book is it said of the Christians, "They loved not their lives unto the death"?

12. Who said, "My people are destroyed for lack of knowledge"?

13. Who wrote, "The just shall live by his faith"?

14. Who said, "Thou hast not lied unto men, but unto God"? To whom did he say it?

15. In what Book is the saying, "A wise son maketh a glad father"?

16. Who said, "Fear ye not, stand still, and see the salvation of the Lord"? To whom was he speaking? On what occasion?

17. Who said, "The Lord thy God is a consuming fire"?

18. Who said, "Blessed art thou among women"? To whom was it said?

19. Who wrote, "Our sufficiency is of God"?

20. Who wrote, "So built we the wall; . . .for the people had a mind to work"?

21. Who wrote, "Cast thy burden upon the Lord, and he shall sustain thee"?

22. Who said, "Even the very hairs of your head are all numbered"?

23. In what Book is the saying, "Ye shall keep my sabbaths, and reverence my sanctuary"?

24. Who offered the prayer, "Hear thou in heaven thy dwelling place: and when thou hearest, forgive"?

25. Who said, "Bring forth therefore fruits meet for repentance"?

SECTION 26

1. Who wrote, "Unto him that loved us, and washed us from our sins in his own blood, and hath made us kings and priests unto God and his Father; to him be glory and dominion for ever and ever"? In what Book?

2. Who wrote about "the chambers of imagery"?
3. Who said of the devil, "He is a liar, and the father of it"?
4. Who prayed, "Wash me, and I shall be whiter than snow"?
5. Who said, "Thy love to me was wonderful, passing the love of women"? Of whom did he say it?
6. In what Book is the saying, "A threefold cord is not quickly broken"?
7. Who wrote, "I determined not to know anything among you, save Jesus Christ, and him crucified"? To whom was he writing?
8. Who wrote, "The lines are fallen unto me in pleasant places; yea, I have a goodly heritage"?
9. Who said, "It is not good that man should be alone"?
10. Where is it said, "The stars in their courses fought against Sisera"?
11. Who wrote, "Wherein thou judgest another, thou condemnest thyself"?
12. Who said, "Go up, thou bald head; go up, thou bald head," and to whom?
13. In what Book does God say, "When thou passest through the waters, I will be with thee"?
14. In what Book does it say, "The Lord is good a strong hold in the day of trouble"?
15. Who wrote, "Awake thou that sleepest, and arise from the dead, and Christ shall give thee light"? In what Book?
16. Who said, "The Spirit of the Lord will come upon thee, and thou shalt be turned into another man"? To whom did he say it?

17. Who was it who denied that he had eaten his morsel alone?

18. In what Book is it said, "Love is strong as death; jealousy is cruel as the grave"?

19. Who said, "If a man keep my saying, he shall never see death"?

20. In what Book is the benediction, "Now unto the king eternal, immoral, invisible, and the only wise God, be honor and glory for ever and ever. Amen"?

21. Who wrote, "The Lord knoweth how to deliver the godly out of temptations"?

22. Where is the sentence, "Wherefore seeing we also are compassed about with so great a cloud of witnesses, let us lay aside every weight, and the sin which doth so easily beset us, and let us run with patience the race that is set before us, looking unto Jesus the author and finisher of our faith; who for the joy that was set before him endured the cross, despising the shame, and is set down at the right hand of the throne of God"?

23. Who said, "The eternal God is thy refuge, and underneath are the everlasting arms"?

24. Who said, "Who knoweth whether thou art come to the kingdom for such a time as this"? and to whom was it said?

25. Who said, "We ought to obey God rather than men"?

SECTION 27

1. Who said, "Wist ye not that I must be about my Father's business"? On what occasion?

2. Who wrote, "The kingdom of God is not in word, but in power"?

3. Who wrote of the heavenly city, "The glory of God did lighten it, and the Lamb is the light thereof"?

4. What is the proverb describing wine as a mocker?

5. Who said, "We do not well: this day is a day of good tidings, and we hold our peace"?

6. Who said, "The Lord hath need of him"? Concerning what?

7. What is Paul's saying about the wages of sin?

8. Who wrote, "The prayer of faith shall save the sick"?

9. What is the verse of the psalm about trusting in chariots?

10. Who said, "I will call upon the Lord, and he shall send thunder and rain"?

11. Who said to his advisers, "No doubt but ye are the people, and wisdom shall die with you"?

12. Who wrote, "Whilst we are at home in the body, we are absent from the Lord"?

13. What ruler asked of Jesus, "What is truth"?

14. In what Book is the prophecy, "I will bring forth my servant the BRANCH"?

15. Who asked his followers to pray for him, "that the word of the Lord may have free course, and be glorified"?

16. On what occasion did the people cry, "The LORD, he is the God; the LORD, he is the God"?

17. What psalm verse did Christ quote on the cross?

18. What saying of Christ's introduces a hen and her chickens?

19. What is Paul's saying about godliness and contentment?

20. Quote Christ's saying about figs and thistles.
21. What is Paul's saying about calling on Christ's name?
22. Who said, "The Father is in me, and I in him"?
23. Quote Paul's hymn of Christian love.
24. Who said, "Be of good courage, and let us play the men of our people, and for the cities of our God: and the LORD do that which seemeth him good"?
25. In what Book is this account of the heavenly city: "There shall in no wise enter into it any thing that defileth, neither whatsoever worketh abomination, or maketh a lie: but they which are written in the Lamb's book of life"?

SECTION 28

1. Quote the advice regarding prosperity and adversity given in Ecclesiastes.
2. Who prophesied, "There shall come a Star out of Jacob, and a Scepter shall rise out of Israel"?
3. Who said, "Though he slay me, yet will I trust him"?
4. Complete John's saying, "In him was life—."
5. Who advised, "Let all things be done decently and in order"?
6. To whom was it said, and about whom, "He is a chosen vessel unto me, to bear my name before the Gentiles"?
7. To what prophet was it said, "I will pour out my spirit upon all flesh; and your sons and your daughters shall prophesy, your old men shall dream dreams, your young men shall see visions"?

8. In what Book is it said, " So we thy people and sheep of thy pasture will give thee thanks forever"?

9. What is the seventh Commandment?

10. Who cried, "Holy, holy, holy, is the LORD of hosts: the whole earth is full of his glory"?

11. Who sung, "Hosanna; Blessed is he that cometh in the name of the Lord"? On what occasion?

12. Finish Paul's saying, "A little leaven—."

13. Who said, "What I have written I have written"? In what connection?

14. Who said, "Here am I; send me"? When?

15. To whom did God say, "Is anything too hard for the LORD"? In what connection?

16. Repeat Ruth's declaration that she would go with Naomi.

17. What did Christ say about turning the other cheek?

18. What is the verse about entertaining angels?

19. How did Paul describe the struggle between what he loved and what he hated?

20. How did Christ sum up His instructions about seeking the best seats at a feast?

21. To whom was it said, "What meanest thou, O sleeper"? On what occasion?

22. What is the conclusion of the verse, "From the rising of the sun unto the going down of the same—."

23. Finish Paul's sentence, "The Lord direct your hearts into the love of God—."

24. Of whom did Christ say, "This sickness is not unto death, but for the glory of God"?

25. What is the proverb about "divers weights and measures"?

SECTION 29

1. What is the proverb about "even a child"?
2. Who said, "By their fruits ye shall know them"?
3. Who said, "Tabitha, arise"?
4. Who said, "I do remember my faults this day"? On what occasion?
5. Where is the saying, "Thine eye shall not pity, but life shall go for life, eye for eye, tooth for tooth, hand for hand, foot for foot"?
6. Who said, "Behold, there ariseth a little cloud out of the sea, like a man's hand"? On what occasion?
7. Who said, "They need not depart; give ye them to eat"?
8. Who said, "As many as I love, I rebuke and chasten: be zealous therefore, and repent"? In what Book?
9. What were Paul's orders about labor?
10. Where is the saying, "Great peace have they which love thy law"?
11. What is the eighth Commandment?
12. Who said, "Is thy servant a dog, that he should do this great thing"?
13. Repeat Ps. 23.
14. Where is the sentence, "I am the rose of Sharon, and the lily of the valleys"?
15. Who said, "The wedding is ready, but they which were bidden were not worthy"?
16. Who asked, "How shall they hear without a preacher?"
17. Where is the saying, "He that is unjust, let him be unjust still"?
18. Who said, "One man of you shall chase a thousand: for the LORD your God, he it is that fighteth for you,

as he hath promised you"?

19. Who said, "How beautiful upon the mountains are the feet of him that bringeth good tidings, that publisheth peace?"

20. Finish the proverb concerning wisdom, "I love them that love me—."

21. Who wrote, "We walk by faith, not by sight"?

22. Who said, "O generation of vipers, who hath warned you to flee from the wrath to come?"

23. Finish Paul's saying, "Be not deceived; God is not mocked—."

24. Who spoke the parable about the poor man's little ewe lamb?

25. When did Christ say, "Woman, behold thy son!"

SECTION 30

1. Where is the prophecy, "In that day. . .shall ye call every man his neighbor under the vine and under the fig tree"?

2. Who said, "It may be that the LORD will work for us: for there is no restraint to the LORD to save by many or by few"?

3. What prophet reported these words from the Lord, "Ye shall seek me, and find me, when ye shall search for me with all your heart"?

4. Finish Paul's saying, "Look not every man on his own things—."

5. Who said, "My house shall be called of all nations the house of prayer, but ye have made it a den of thieves"?

6. In what Book is the prophecy, "Behold, a virgin shall

conceive, and bear a son, and shall call his name Immanuel"?

7. Of whom if it said that he "became mighty, because he prepared his ways before the LORD his God"?

8. Who said, "The love of money is the root of all evil"?

9. What is the ninth Commandment?

10. Who said, "Man that is born of a woman is of few days, and full of trouble"?

11. What is the first part of the saying which ends, "Let us go on unto perfection"?

12. What is the saying about "effectual fervent prayer"?

13. What is Christ's saying about "the highways and hedges"?

14. Who said, "Thou are the man"? And to whom did he say it?

15. Finish the verse of the psalm which begins, "The earth is the LORD's."

16. Who said, "All thy billows and thy waves passed over me"?

17. Who wrote, "Christ our passover is sacrificed for us"?

18. Finish John's saying, "The law was given by Moses, but—."

19. Who said to Moses, "Ye have compassed this mountain long enough"?

20. Who asked, "Friend, how camest thou in hither not having a wedding garment"?

21. To whom did the Lord say, "What God hath cleansed, that call not thou common"?

22. What prophet cried, "Multitudes, multitudes, in the valley of decision"?

23. Who said, "It is not in me: God shall give Pharaoh

an answer of peace"?

24. Who said, "To obey is better than sacrifice," and to whom did he say it?

25. Who said, "We have toiled all the night, and have taken nothing: nevertheless at thy word I will let down the net"?

SECTION 31

1. Who said, "This day I am going the way of all the earth"?

2. What is the proverb about bargaining?

3. What prophet wrote, "Not by might, nor by power, but by my spirit, saith the LORD of hosts"?

4. What is Christ's saying about the second mile?

5. Of whom was it said, "These that have turned the world upside down are come hither also"?

6. Who wrote, "Let this mind be in you, which was also in Christ Jesus"?

7. Who asked, "If a man die, shall he live again"? and what did he add?

8. What is the tenth Commandment?

9. Of whom was it said, "He driveth furiously"?

10. What is the first part of the sentence, ending, "from whence cometh my help"?

11. Finish Isaiah's sentence, "The people that walked in darkness—."

12. Who said, "Touch me not," and to whom?

13. Whom did Paul exhort, "Fight the good fight of faith"?

14. Finish the verse in Revelation, "Behold, I stand at the door, and knock"?

15. To whom did the Lord say, "I have loved thee with an everlasting love"?

16. What is the conclusion of Christ's sentence, "Not every one that saith unto me, Lord, Lord, shall enter into the kingdom of heaven—"?

17. What does James say about the rewards for converting sinners?

18. How does Amos describe the oppressions of the rich?

19. Who said, "Shall not the Judge of all the earth do right"? On what occasion?

20. Where is it said, "God hath made man upright; but they have sought out many inventions"?

21. Who said, "Be of good cheer; it is I; be not afraid"?

22. Who cried, "O wretched man that I am! who shall deliver me from the body of this death?"

23. Who wrote of Christ, "Whom having not seen, ye love; in whom, though now ye see him not, yet believing , ye rejoice with joy unspeakable and full of glory"?

24. Finish the verse of the psalm beginning, "I love the LORD, because—."

25. In what Book is the verse, "He brought me to the banqueting house, and his banner over me was love"?

SECTION 32

1. Complete Christ's saying, "What things soever ye desire, when ye pray—."

2. What is Paul's sentence linking together "faith" and "hearing"?

3. What is the invitation verse of the Revelation?

4. Who said, "With him is an arm of flesh; but with us

is the LORD our God to help us, and to fight our battles." Of what enemy was he speaking?

5. What is the proverb about sinning against wisdom?

6. Who said, "Many are called, but few are chosen"?

7. Who wrote, "Christ died for our sins according to the scriptures"?

8. Finish the statement in Hebrews, that Christ was made, "not after the law of a carnal commandment, but—."

9. What is the psalm verse about "the finest of the wheat"?

10. Who said, "Behold the Lamb of God, which taketh away the sin of the world"?

11. Who wrote, "The love of Christ constraineth us"?

12. What is the last verse of the Bible?

13. What does Deuteronomy say about paying vows?

14. Finish the psalm verse beginning, "Justice and judgment are the habitation of thy thone—."

15. What does Paul say about being weary in well doing?

16. To whom did Christ say, "I am the resurrection and the life"?

17. What metaphor does Paul use regarding baptism?

18. How does the psalmist express his longing for God's house?

19. Who wrote, "Be not weary in well doing"?

20. What prophet asks, "Can two walk together, except they be agreed"?

21. Where is it said, "Marriage is honourable in all"?

22. Who said, "This city is near to flee unto, and it is a little one: Oh, let me escape thither, (is it not a little one?) and my soul shall live"?

23. What did Christ say about hating one's own family?

24. What is Paul's "no condemnation" verse?

25. What did Christ say about lending?

SECTION 33

1. Who asked, "Can we find such a one as this is, a man in whom the Spirit of God is"?
2. Who said, "Thou hast rejected the word of the LORD, and the LORD hath rejected thee from being king over Israel"? To whom was he speaking?
3. What was Christ's answer when the leper said, "Lord if thou wilt, thou canst make me clean"?
4. In what Book did the expression, "Touch not; taste not; handle not," originate?
5. Who wrote, "The gifts and calling of God are without repentance"?
6. On what great occasion did Christ say, "Peace be unto you"?
7. Finish Isaiah's sentence, "They shall see eye to eye—."
8. Who said, "Fear not: for God is come to prove you, and that his fear may be before your faces, that ye sin not"? When?
9. Complete the verse of the psalm, "Blessed is the people that know the joyful sound—."
10. Who cried, "Yet forty days, and Nineveh shall be overthrown"?
11. Who said to Christ, "Depart from me, for I am a sinful man, O Lord"? When?
12. Finish Paul's sentence, "As we have therefore opportunity—."
13. Who said, "Miserable comforters are ye all"? To whom?
14. In what Book is the command, "Thou shalt not

muzzle the ox when he treadeth out the corn"?

15. What verse in Isaiah contains five titles of Christ?

16. What was Christ's decision in regard to paying taxes to the Romans?

17. Who said, "Stand up; I myself also am a man"? On what occasion?

18. What is Paul's advice to the rich?

19. To whom did Christ say, "O thou of little faith, wherefore didst thou doubt"? On what occasion?

20. What prophet asked, "Who hath despised the day of small things"?

21. When was it said of Manasseh that he "knew that the LORD he was God"?

22. Finish the psalm verse: "The LORD is thy keeper—"

23. Who said, "God hath made me to laugh, so that all that hear will laugh with me"? On what occasion?

24. Who wrote, "I will put my law in their inward parts, and write it in their hearts"?

25. What did Christ say about marriage in heaven?

SECTION 1

1. Nebuchadnezzar. Dan. 4:28, 30.
2. "To leave the other undone." Luke 11:42.
3. Elihu. Job 32:6, 7.
4. Moses. Ex. 14:13, 14.
5. Ps. 100:1. "Make a joyful noise unto the LORD, all ye lands."
6. Said by the angel to Zacharias, of John the Baptist.
7. Rev. 13:8.
8. Gamaliel. Acts 5:37-39.
9. Adam. Gen. 2:24.
10. "Ye shall be free indeed." John 8:36.
11. The Lord. Lev. 24:20.
12. The tongue. Jas. 3:8.
13. "Thee to repentance." Rom. 2:4.
14. "By prayer and fasting." Mark 9:29.
15. Paul. Titus 2:13.
16. David. Ps. 15:4
17. Nehemiah. Neh. 4:14.
18. Solomon's Song 8:7.
19. God, at Christ's baptism. Matt. 3:17.
20. Paul. Eph. 5:16.
21. God, speaking to Isaiah. Isa. 42:4.
22. "A word spoken in due season." Prov. 15:23.
23. "The things which God hath prepared for them that love him." 1 Cor. 2:9.
24. Christ. Matt. 12:36.
25. "Your sanctification." 1 Thess. 4:3.

SECTION 2

1. "Consent thou not," Prov. 1:10.
2. John the Baptist's. Matt. 3:10.
3. God, speaking to Jeremiah. Jer. 6:14.
4. "Honor thy father and mother." Eph. 6:2.
5. David. Ps. 56:8.
6. Adam. Gen. 3:12.
7. Habakkuk. Hab. 1:13.
8. The Pharisees. Luke 11:43.
9. "Surely in vain the net is spread in the sight of any bird." Prov. 1:17.
10. Solomon. 1 Chron. 28:9.
11. The Virgin Mary. Luke 1:38.
12. "The things of the Spirit of God." 1 Cor. 2:14.
13. "Enter into his gates with thanksgiving." Ps. 100:4.
14. Saul. 1 Sam. 10:11.
15. Job. Job 38:2.
16. "Bring my sons from far, and my daughters from the ends of the earth." Isa. 43:6.
17. "If the salt have lost his saltness, wherewith will ye season it?" Mark 9:50.
18. "He is able to succor them that are tempted." Heb. 2:18.
19. "Thou shalt find him, if thou seek him with all thy heart and with all thy soul." Deut. 4:29.
20. "Before Abraham was, I am." John 8:58.
21. "There is no respect of persons with God." Rom. 2:11.
22. "Pride goeth before destruction, and an haughty spirit before a fall." Prov. 16:18.
23. "And none shall make you afraid." Lev. 26:6.

24. Ps. 61:2.
25. Daniel to Belshazzar. Dan. 5:17.

SECTION 3

1. Moses. Ex. 14:15.
2. Mary's. Luke 1:52.
3. "The letter killeth, but the spirit giveth life." 2 Cor. 3:6.
4. "And a thousand years as one day." 2 Pet. 3:8.
5. "Than that thou shouldest vow and not pay." Eccl. 5:5.
6. Deut. 6:4.
7. Job. Job 2:10.
8. "The fathers have eaten sour grapes, and the children's teeth are set on edge." Ezek. 18:2.
9. "Whosoever shall do the will of my Father which is in heaven." Matt. 12:50.
10. By faith in Christ Jesus." Gal. 3:26.
11. "Blessed are the dead which die in the Lord from henceforth: Yea, saith the Spirit, that they may rest from their labours; and their works do follow them." Rev. 14:13.
12. "Pleasant words are as an honeycomb, sweet to the soul, and health to the bones." Prov. 16:24.
13. "My expectation is from him." Ps. 62:5.
14. To Adam, by God. Gen 3:19.
15. "And of Gideon." Judg. 7:18.
16. The apostles. Acts. 6:4.
17. Christ. Mark 10:9.
18. "Unto thee shall all flesh come." Ps. 65:2.

19. Nehemiah. Neh. 6:3.
20. "Lean not unto thine own understanding." Prov. 3:5.
21. "As a thief in the night." 1 Thess. 5:2.
22. The Old Testament men and women of faith. Heb. 11:38.
23. "Ephraim is joined to idols: let him alone." Hos. 4:17.
24. "Learn to do well." Isa. 1:16, 17.
25. "The night cometh, when no man can work." John 9:4.

SECTION 4

1. "Teachest thou not thyself?" Rom. 2:21.
2. Esther. Esth. 4:16.
3. "And he will direct thy paths." Prov. 3:6.
4. David, of Abner. 2 Sam. 3:38.
5. "Whosoever shall confess me before men, him shall the Son of man also confess before the angels of God." Luke 12:8.
6. "And thy paths drop fatness." Ps. 65:11.
7. Moses, after the passage of the Red Sea. Ex. 15.11.
8. "And stablisheth a city by iniquity!" Hab. 2:12.
9. "I am the light of the world." John 9:5.
10. "While it is called To day." Heb. 3:13.
11. James. Jas. 3:18.
12. Isaiah. Isa. 44:22.
13. "Slow to anger, and plenteous in mercy." Ps. 103:8.
14. The Shunammite. 2 Kings 4:12, 13.
15. Paul. 1 Cor. 3:6.
16. Job. Job 3:17.
17. God, of Christ, at His baptism. Matt. 3:17.

18. "Always in a good thing." Gal. 4:18.
19. Stephen, before the Sanhedrin. Acts 7:22.
20. "If it be found in the way of righteousness." Prov. 16:31.
21. Jeremiah. Jer. 8:20.
22. "Ye cannot serve God and mammon." Matt. 6:24.
23. The Revelation. Rev. 1:11.
24. Daniel's, to Belshazzar. Dan. 5:27.
25. "So far hath he removed our transgressions from us." Ps. 103:12.

SECTION 5

1. "Striving against sin." Heb. 12:4.
2. Stephen. Acts. 7:48.
3. Cain. Gen. 4:9.
4. Moses. Deut. 34:7.
5. "And renew a right spirit within me." Ps. 51:10.
6. "To come unto me, and forbid them not: for of such is the kingdom of God." Mark 10:14.
7. Christ. Rev. 1:18.
8. "He correcteth." Prov. 3:12.
9. The queen of Sheba, concerning Solomon's wisdom and splendor. 1 Kings 10:7.
10. "In thy presence is fulness of joy; at the right hand there are pleasures for evermore." Ps. 16:11.
11. "And the body than raiment?" Matt. 6:25.
12. Paul. Rom. 3:4.
13. Jeremiah. Jer. 8:22.
14. The Lord, to Job. Job 38:7.
15. Nehemiah. Neh. 6:11.

16. The man born blind whom Christ healed. John 9:25.
17. "Blessed be the Lord, who daily loadeth us with benefits." Ps. 68:19.
18. Cain. Gen. 4:13.
19. Paul. 1 Tim. 2:5.
20. Christ, to Peter and Andrew. Matt. 4:19.
21. Hosea. Hos. 6:3.
22. "In the abundance of the things which he possesseth." Luke 12:15.
23. Ezekiel. Ezek. 18:20.
24. Joshua. Josh. 1:7.
25. "As the waters cover the sea." Hab. 2:14.

SECTION 6

1. "The zeal of thine house hath eaten me up." Ps. 69:9; John 2:17.
2. "I desired mercy, and not sacrifice; and the knowledge of God more than burnt offerings." Hos. 6:6.
3. "Whom the Lord loveth he chasteneth, and scourgeth every son whom he receiveth." Heb. 12:6.
4. "Enoch walked with God: and he was not; for God took him." Gen. 5:24.
5. Isaiah. Isa. 45:9.
6. "And in her left hand riches and honor." Prov. 3;16.
7. The rich young ruler. Luke 18:18.
8. "There is liberty." 2 Cor. 3:17.
9. Rev. 15:3.
10. "And my mouth shall shew forth thy praise." Ps. 51:15.
11. Miriam's, after the crossing of the Red Sea. Ex. 15:21.

12. Joshua. Josh. 1:8.
13. Jeremiah, "the weeping prophet." Jer. 9:1.
14. Habakkuk. Hab. 2:15.
15. "For theirs is the kingdom of heaven." Matt. 5:3.
16. "Stand fast therefore in the liberty wherewith Christ hath made us free, and be not entangled again with the yoke of bondage." Gal. 5:1.
17. The public Bible reading of Ezra and Nehemiah. Neh. 8:8.
18. Gideon's. Judg. 8:4.
19. "Like as a father pitieth his children, so the Lord pitieth them that fear him." Ps. 103:13.
20. In the parable of the foolish rich man. Luke 12:19.
21. "Faith which worketh by love." Gal. 5:6.
22. "Reap the same." Job 4:8.
23. Ezekiel. Ezek. 18:31.
24. "He that entereth not by the door into the sheepfold, but climeth up some other way, the same is a thief and a robber." John 10:1.
25. "Wisdom is the principal thing; therefore get wisdom: and with all thy getting get understanding." Prov. 4:7.

SECTION 7

1. "Consider the lilies of the field, how they grow; they toil not, neither do they spin: And yet I say unto you, That even Solomon in all his glory was not arrayed like one of these." Matt. 6:29.
2. "But is longsuffering to us-ward, not willing that any should perish, but that all should come to repentance." 2 Peter 3:9.

3. Esther. Esth. 5:6.
4. "All thine heart, and with all thy soul, and with all thy might." Deut. 6:5.
5. "A friend loveth at all times." Prov. 17:17.
6. "And they shall reap the whirlwind." Hos. 8:7.
7. "Putting on the breastplate of faith and love; and for an helmet, the hope of salvation." 1 Thess. 5:8.
8. "Though your sins be as scarlet, they shall be as white as snow; though they be red like crimson, they shall be as wool." Isa. 1:18.
9. The Virgin Mary. Luke 1:53.
10. Paul. Rom. 3:10.
11. "Be filled with the Spirit." Eph. 5:18.
12. "Keep me as the apple of the eye, hide me under the shadow of thy wings." Ps. 17:8.
13. David. 2 Sam. 5:24.
14. God. Job 38:11.
15. King Darius's. Dan. 6:8.
16. "Ye are God's husbandry, ye are God's building." 1 Cor. 3:9.
17. "For they shall be comforted." Matt. 5:4.
18. Of King Saul. 1 Sam. 10:27.
19. God, before the flood. Gen. 6:3.
20. Elisha, of the Shunammite. 2 Kings 4:26.
21. Eccl. 5:9.
22. Christ. Matt. 13:9.
23. "The church of the living God, the pillar and ground of the truth." 1 Tim. 3:15.
24. David. 1 Chron. 29:14.
25. "We hold the beginning of our confidence stedfast unto the end." Heb. 3:14.

SECTION 8

1. "Nevertheless afterward it yieldeth the peaceable fruit of righteousness." Heb. 12:11.
2. Rehoboam, son of Solomon. 1 Kings 12:10.
3. James. Jas. 4:3.
4. Moses. Num. 10:35.
5. That of Ephesus. Rev. 2:4.
6. The Israelites. Lev. 26:8.
7. "The path of the just is as the shining light, that shineth more and more unto the perfect day." Prov. 4:18.
8. "All the ends of the earth." Isa. 45:22.
9. "Blessed are the meek: for they shall inherit the earth." Matt. 5:5.
10. "And come short of the glory of God." Rom. 3:23.
11. "A merry heart doeth good like a medicine." Prov. 17:22.
12. God, to Ezekiel. Ezek. 21:27.
13. King Ahasuerus. Esth. 6:6.
14. "To give the light of knowledge of the glory of God in the face of Jesus Christ." 2 Cor. 4:6.
15. Of John the Baptist. Luke 1:66.
16. Isaiah. Isa. 2:4.
17. Ezra. Neh. 8:10.
18. Moses. Num. 12:3.
19. Job. Job 38:31.
20. "And all these things shall be added unto you." Matt. 6:33.
21. Rev. 16:16.
22. Paul. 1 Thess. 5:10.
23. "A broken spirit: a broken and a contrite heart, O

God, thou wilt not despise." Ps. 51:17.
24. The manna. Ex. 16:15.
25. Zacharias. Luke 1:78.

SECTION 9

1. "Whosoever hath not, from hi shall be taken away even that he hath." Matt. 13:12.
2. "He shall be saved, and shall go in and out, and find pasture." John 10:9.
3. "And the little hills, by righteousness." Ps. 72:3.
4. Of the days before the flood. Gen. 6:4.
5. Heb. 3:15.
6. Stephen. Acts 7:56.
7. The rich young ruler. Luke 18:22.
8. Hosea. Hos. 10:13.
9. That he "shall not be satisfied with silver." Eccl. 5:10.
10. "The Lord is my rock, and my fortress, and my deliverer; my God, my strength, in whom I will trust; my buckler, and the horn of my salvation, and my high tower." Ps. 18:2.
11. Solomon. 2 Chron. 1:8, 10.
12. "They shall be filled". Matt. 5:6.
13. "Other foundation can no man lay than that is laid, which is Jesus Christ." 1 Cor. 3:11.
14. "Keep thy heart with all diligence; for out of it are the issues of life." Prov. 4:23.
15. David. 2 Sam. 6:9.
16. "Thou shalt bind them for a sign upon thine hand, and they shall be as frontlets between thine eyes." Deut. 6:8.
17. Jeremiah. Jer. 10:23.

18. "Ye fathers, provoke not your children to wrath: but bring them up in the nurture and admonition of the Lord." Eph. 6:4.

19. The church in Smyrna. Rev. 2:8, 10.

20. "Be strong and of a good courage; be not afraid, neither be thou dismayed: for the Lord thy God is with thee withersoever thou goest." Josh. 1:9.

21. Daniel. Dan. 6:22.

22. Christ. Luke 12:30.

23. Paul. 1 Tim. 3:16.

24. "We, according to his promise, look for new heavens and a new earth, wherein dwelleth righteousness." 2 Pet. 3:13.

25. "As for man, his days are as grass: as a flower of the field, so he flourisheth." Ps. 103:15.

SECTION 10

1. To Elisha. 2 Kings 4:38, 40.

2. "Shall a man be more pure than his maker?" Job 4:17.

3. "Let all the earth keep silence before him." Hab. 2:20.

4. "Blessed are the merciful: for they shall obtain mercy." Matt. 5:7.

5. "A little leaven leaveneth the whole lump." Gal. 5:9.

6. "God resisteth the proud, but giveth grace unto the humble." Jas. 4:6.

7. "Drink waters out of thine own cistern, and running waters out of thine own well." Prov. 5:15.

8. "He sent from above, he took me." Ps. 18:16.

9. Rehoboam, son of Solomon. 1 Kings 12:6, 11.

10. Christ. Matt. 13:16.

11. Paul. 1 Thess. 5:15.

12. Saul. 1 Sam. 11:13.
13. "And the feeble knees; and make straight paths for your feet." Heb. 12:12, 13.
14. Jephthah. Judg. 11:31.
15. "Even to your old age I am he; and even to hoar hairs will I carry you." Isa. 46:4.
16. Stephen. Acts 7:59.
17. The parable of the sower. Matt. 13:21.
18. "Is counted wise." Prov. 17:28.
19. God, after the flood. Gen. 8:22.
20. Samuel. 1 Sam. 12:1, 3.
21. Rev. 19:6.
22. Paul. Rom. 4:25.
23. "Upon them that fear him, and his righteousness unto children's children." Ps. 103:17.
24. The manna. Ex. 16:18.
25. "The inspiration of the Almighty giveth them understanding." Job 32:8.

SECTION 11

1. "With bands of love." Hos. 11:4.
2. "The good shepherd giveth his life for the sheep." John 10:11.
3. Rev. 2:17.
4. Joshua. Josh. 3:8.
5. "And his kingdom ruleth over all." Ps. 103:19.
6. "Take therefore no thought for the morrow: for the morrow shall take thought for the things of itself. Sufficient unto the day is the evil thereof." Matt. 6:34.
7. "Every creature of God is good, and nothing to be refused, if it be received with thanksgiving." 1 Tim. 4:4.

8. The ten cowardly spies. Num. 13:28.
9. The prayer of the Levites. Neh. 9:5, 17.
10. "Blessed are the pure in heart, for they shall see God." Matt. 5:8.
11. "The fire shall try every man's work of what sort it is." 1 Cor. 3:13.
12. The heroes of faith of the Old Testament. Heb. 11:34.
13. Deut. 6:9.
14. "The fool hath said in his heart, "There is no God." Ps. 53:1.
15. "Yet I will rejoice in the Lord, I will joy in the God of my salvation." Hab. 3:17, 18.
16. "So is he that layeth up treasure for himself, and is not rich toward God." Luke 12:21.
17. "He will flee from you." Jas. 4:7.
18. An Ephraimite. Judg. 12:5, 6.
19. Isaiah's. Isa. 2:5.
20. "How hard is it for them that trust in riches to enter into the kingdom of God!" Mark 10:24.
21. Paul. 1 Thess. 5:16.
22. Jeremiah. Jer. 13:23.
23. "And envy slayeth the silly one." Job 5:2.
24. "They are increased that eat them." Eccl. 5:11.
25. Stephen. Acts 7:60.

SECTION 12

1. Of Mary and Joseph. Luke 2:7.
2. Solomon in dedicating the temple. 2 Chron. 6:13, 18.
3. Noah and his sons. Gen. 9:1, 6.
4. "He shall judge the poor of the people, he shall save the children of the needy, and shall break in pieces

the oppressor." Ps. 72:4.

5. "Go to the ant, thou sluggard; consider her ways, and be wise." Prov. 6:6.

6. "Yet the inward man is renewed day by day." 2 Cor. 4:16.

7. John. 1 John 1:5.

8. The king of Israel, when Naaman came to be cured of leprosy. 2 Kings 5:7.

9. Ezekiel, on the death of his wife. Ezek. 24:16.

10. "Judge not, that ye be not judged." Matt. 7:1.

11. "Thou shalt love thy neighbor as thyself." Gal. 5:14.

12. Job. Job 42:5.

13. Obed-edom. 2 Sam. 6:12.

14. "Not with eyeservice, as menpleasers; but as servants of Christ, doing the will of God from the heart." Eph. 6:6.

15. "Blessed are the peacemakers: for they shall be called the children of God." Matt. 5:9.

16. "For thou wilt light my candle: the Lord my God will enlighten my darkness." Ps. 18:28.

17. Jeroboam and his followers. 1 Kings 12:12, 16.

18. Paul. 1 Thess. 5:17.

19. Dan. 7:22, and elsewhere in Daniel.

20. "Because of unbelief." Heb. 3:19.

21. Caleb. Num. 13:30.

22. "Or who is a rock save our God?" Ps. 18:31.

23. "Even so know I the Father." John 10:15.

24. "Therefore being justified by faith, we have peace with God through our Lord Jesus Christ." Rom 5:1.

25. Zeph. 3:17.

SECTION 13

1. David. 2 Sam. 6:14.
2. "Blessed are they which are persecuted for right-eousness' sake: for theirs is the kingdom of heaven." Matt. 5:10.
3. "Know ye not that ye are the temple of God, and that the Spirit of God dwelleth in you?" 1 Cor. 3:16.
4. Dan. 12:2.
5. "For it is your Father's good pleasure to give you the kingdom." Luke 12:32.
6. Rev. 19:9.
7. "And the Lord alone shall be exalted in that day." Isa. 2:11.
8. Nehemiah. Neh. 13:11.
9. "It is easier for a camel to go through the eye of a nee-dle, than for a rich man to enter into the kingdom of God." Mark 10:25.
10. Simon the sorcerer. Acts 8:9, 10.
11. "Yet a little sleep, a little slumber, a little folding of the hands to sleep: so shall thy poverty come as one that travelleth, and thy want as an armed man." Prov. 6:10, 11.
12. Jethro, Moses' father-in-law, after the exodus. Ex. 18:10, 11.
13. "The sparks fly upward." Job 5:7.
14. "As to the Lord, and not to men." Eph. 6:7.
15. "Other sheep I have, which are not of this fold: them also I must bring." John 10:16.
16. "And whose heart departeth from the Lord." Jer. 17:5.
17. "I do set my bow in the cloud, and it shall be for a token of a covenant between me and the earth."

Gen. 9:13.

18. "Walk in the Spirit, and ye shall not fulfil the lust of the flesh." Gal. 5:16.

19. "If we walk in the light, as he is in the light, we have fellowship one with another, and the blood of Jesus Christ his son cleanseth us from all sin." 1 John 1:7.

20. "We have this treasure in earthen vessels, that the excellency of the power may be of God, and not of us." 2 Cor. 4:7.

21. "And the firmament sheweth his handywork." Ps. 19:1.

22. "The righteous runneth into it, and is safe." Prov. 18:10.

23. King Asa. 2 Chron. 14:11.

24. Isa. 48:22.

25. To the shepherds at Bethlehem. Luke 2:10.

SECTION 14

1. "The care of this world, and the deceitfulness of riches, choke the word, and he becometh unfruitful. Matt. 13:22.

2. Paul. 1 Thess. 5:18.

3. Ezekiel. Ezek. 33:9.

4. "He shall come down like rain upon the mown grass: as showers that water the earth." Ps. 72:6.

5. Deut. 6:16.

6. "Why beholdest thou the mote that is in thy brother's eye, but considerest not the beam that is in thine own eye?" Matt. 7:3.

7. "Bodily exercise profiteth little: but godliness is profitable unto all things, having promise of the life that

now is, and of that which is to come." 1 Tim. 4:8.

8. Naaman's servants. 2 Kings 5:13.

9. "The sleep of a labouring man is sweet, whether he eat little or much: but the abundance of the rich will not suffer him to sleep." Eccl. 5:12.

10. Moses. Ex. 19:4.

11. Joshua's cairn commemorating the passage of the Jordan. Josh. 4:21.

12. That of Sardis. Rev. 3:1.

13. Ps. 104:16.

14. Samson. Judg. 14:14.

15. "And from the river unto the ends of the earth." Ps. 72:8.

16. Christ. Matt. 5:13.

17. "To the people of God." Heb. 4:9.

18. Elijah. 1 Kings 17:1, 4.

19. Heb. 12:14.

20. "In wisdom hast thou made them all." Ps. 104:24.

21. "Where your treasure is, there will your heart be also." Luke 12:34.

22. "And he will draw nigh to you." Jas. 4:8.

23. Haggai. Hag. 1:4.

24. "I will sing praise to my God while I have my being." Ps. 104:33.

25. Jeremiah. Jer. 17:7.

SECTION 15

1. "Our light affliction, which is but for a moment, worketh for us a far more exceeding and eternal weight of glory." 2 Cor. 4:17.

2. "Be ye therefore ready also: for the Son of man

cometh in an hour when ye think not." Luke 12:40.

3. Isaiah. Isa. 2:22.
4. Nehemiah. Neh. 13:17.
5. Paul. Eph. 6:10.
6. Christ. Mark 10:27.
7. Nimrod. Gen 10:9.
8. "The testimony of the Lord is sure, making wise the simple." Ps. 19:7.
9. Ezekiel. Ezek. 33:11.
10. Paul's. 1 Thess. 5:19.
11. "That they may see your good works, and glorify your Father which is in heaven." Matt. 5:16.
12. Azariah. 2 Chron. 15:2.
13. To the Israelites, through Moses. Ex. 19:3, 6.
14. Heb. 12:23.
15. Simon the sorcerer. Acts 8:18, 20.
16. Christ. John 10:16.
17. "And forsake not the law of thy mother." Prov. 6:20.
18. "Despise not thou the chastening of the Almighty." Job 5:17.
19. "He shall lift you up." Jas. 4:10.
20. An angel, speaking to the shepherds. Luke 2:11.
21. Isaiah. Isa. 49:6.
22. Hosea. Hos. 13:14.
23. Paul. Rom. 5:3, 4.
24. Christ. Matt. 13:29.
25. Eccl. 6:7.

SECTION 16

1. "I have power to lay it down, and I have power to take it again." John 10:18.

2. To Moses at Sinai. Ex. 19:8.
3. "The poor also, and him that hath no helper." Ps. 72:12.
4. That it is "foolishness with God." 1 Cor. 3:19.
5. "We deceive ourselves, and the truth is not in us." 1 John 1:8.
6. "Humility." Prov. 18:12.
7. At the building of the Tower of Babel. Gen. 11:4.
8. Isaiah. Isa. 3:24.
9. "Give not that which is holy unto the dogs, neither cast ye your pearls before swine." Matt. 7:6.
10. Timothy. 1 Tim. 4:12.
11. Philadelphia. Rev. 3:7, 8.
12. "All nations shall call him blessed." Ps. 72:17.
13. At the beginning of the Ten Commandments. Ex. 20:2.
14. "They that be wise shall shine as the brightness of the firmament; and they that turn many to righteousness as the stars for ever and ever." Dan. 12:3.
15. Christ. Mark 10:31.
16. "In due time Christ died for the ungodly." Rom. 5:6.
17. "The word of God is quick, and powerful, and sharper than any twoedged sword, piercing even to the dividing asunder of soul and spirit, and of the joints and marrow, and is a discerner of the thoughts and intents of the heart." Heb. 4:12.
18. "Who walk in the law of the LORD." Ps. 119:1.
19. Naaman. 2 Kings 5:17, 18.
20. "He that earneth wages earneth wages to put it into a bag with holes." Hag. 1:6.
21. Christ. Luke 12:48.
22. "The flesh lusteth against the Spirit, and the Spirit

against the flesh: and these are contrary the one to the other: so that ye cannot do the things that ye would." Gal. 5:17.

23. The widow of Zarephath. 1 Kings 17:9, 14.
24. Joshua and Caleb. Num. 14:6, 9.
25. John, in the Revelation. Rev. 19:16.

SECTION 17

1. Moses. Deut. 8:2.
2. The angels, at Bethlehem. Luke 2:14.
3. Paul. Rom 5:8.
4. His wife Michal. 2 Sam. 6:20.
5. "Death and life are in the power of the tongue." Prov. 18:21.
6. "Ask, and it shall be given to you; seek, and ye shall find; knock, and it shall be opened unto you." Matt. 7:7.
7. Samson. Judg. 14:18.
8. "By taking heed thereto according to thy word." Ps. 119:9.
9. "For what is your life? It is even a vapor, that appeareth for a little time, and then vanisheth away." Jas. 4:14.
10. The man with a drawn sword, to Joshua. Josh. 5:13, 14.
11. Isaiah. Isa. 49:10.
12. Christ. Luke 12:50.
13. "Hold fast that which is good." 1 Thess. 5:21.
14. "Thou shalt have no other gods before me." Ex. 20:3.
15. "My days are swifter than a weaver's shuttle, and

are spent without hope." Job 7:6.

16. "More to be desired are they than gold, yea, than much fine gold: sweeter also than honey and the honeycomb." Ps. 19:10.

17. James and John. Mark 10:35, 38.

18. "We look not at the things which are seen, but at the things which are not seen: for the things which are seen are temporal; but the things which are not seen are eternal." 2 Cor. 4:18.

19. "I saw a new heaven and a new earth: for the first heaven and the first earth were passed away; and there was no more sea." Rev. 21:1.

20. "Say unto him, Take away all iniquity, and receive us graciously: so will we render the calves of our lips." Hos. 14:2.

21. "And afterward receive me to glory." Ps. 73:24.

22. "For righteousness, but behold a cry." Isa. 5:7.

23. How much more shall your Father which is in heaven give good things to them that ask him?" Matt. 7:11.

24. "All are yours; and ye are Christ's; and Christ is God's. 1 Cor. 3:22, 23.

25. Peter, to Simon the scorcerer. Acts 8:23.

SECTION 18

1. "It is better to go to the house of mourning, than to go to the house of feasting: for that is the end of all men; and the living will lay it to his heart." Eccl. 7:2.

2. Abraham. Gen. 12:1, 2.

3. "My sheep hear my voice, and I know them, and

they follow me." John 10:27.

4. Timothy. 1 Tim. 4:14.

5. "That I might not sin against thee." Ps. 119:11.

6. "Thou shalt not make unto thee any graven image," etc. Ex. 20:4-6.

7. Deut. 8:18.

8. "And his clothes not be burned?" Prov. 6:27.

9. The parable of the tares. Matt. 13:43.

10. "So by the obedience of one shall many be made righteous." Rom. 5:19.

11. "To him it is sin." Jas. 4:17.

12. Simeon, when Jesus was presented in the temple. Luke 2:29.

13. "The heart is deceitful above all things, and desperately wicked: who can know it?" Jer. 17:9.

14. Moses, at Meribah. Num. 20:10, 13.

15. "A man that hath friends must shew himself friendly: and there is a friend that sticketh closer than a brother." Prov. 18:24.

16. "Till heaven and earth pass, one jot or one tittle shall in no wise pass from the law, till all be fulfilled." Matt. 5:18.

17. "Love, joy, peace, longsuffering, gentleness, goodness, faith, meekness, temperance." Gal. 5:22, 23.

18. "I will shake all nations, and the desire of all nations shall come: and I will fill this house with glory." Hag. 2:7.

19. The girdle of truth, the breastplate of righteousness, the sandals of peace, the shield of faith, the helmet of salvation, and "the sword of the Spirit, which is the word of God." Eph. 6:13-17.

20. "I will take away the stony heart out of your flesh,

and I will give you an heart of flesh." Ezek. 36:26.

21. Job. Job 7:16.
22. "And filleth the hungry soul with goodness." Ps. 107:9.
23. Samson. Judg. 15:16.
24. Heb. 4:15.
25. Laodicea. Rev. 3:14, 16.

SECTION 19

1. "In the beginning was the Word, and the Word was with God, and the Word was God." John 1:1.
2. Amos. Amos 8:5.
3. King Ahab to Elijah. 1 Kings 18:17.
4. "He is faithful and just to forgive us our sins, and to cleanse us from all unrighteousness." 1 John 1:9.
5. Hanani. 2 Chron. 16:7, 9.
6. Joshua, referring to Jericho. Josh. 6:2, 16.
7. Heb. 12:29.
8. Christ. John 18:36.
9. Elisha, speaking to Gehazi. 2 Kings 5:25, 27.
10. Joseph's brothers, referring to Joseph. Gen. 37:17, 19.
11. "Let the words of my mouth, and the meditation of my heart, be acceptable in thy sight, O Lord, my strength, and my redeemer." Ps. 19:14.
12. Christ. Luke 13:3.
13. Paul. Phil. 1:21.
14. Rev. 21:4.
15. Job. Job 9:2.
16. "Thou shalt not take the name of the Lord thy God in vain." Ex. 20:7.

17. Moses. Deut. 11:26.
18. Isaiah. Isa. 5:21.
19. "If thy right eye offend thee, pluck it out, and cast it from thee." Matt. 5:29.
20. "Reckon ye also yourselves to be dead indeed unto sin, but alive unto God through Jesus Christ our Lord." Rom. 6:11.
21. "Bind them upon thy fingers, write them upon the table of thine heart." Prov. 7:3.
22. "God is the strength of my heart, and my portion for ever." Ps. 73:26.
23. "But to minister, and to give his life a ransom for many." Mark 10:45.
24. Hosea. Hos. 14:4.
25. "I may behold wondrous things out of thy law." Ps. 119:18.

SECTION 20

1. Christ. Matt. 5:34.
2. Paul. 1 Tim. 5:8.
3. Simeon, of the Virgin Mary. Luke 2:34, 35.
4. David. Ps. 20:5.
5. Abraham, to Lot. Gen. 13:8, 9.
6. Micaiah. 2 Chron. 18:7.
7. Jeremiah. Jer. 17:14.
8. "To this end was I born, and for this cause came I into the world, that I should bear witness unto the truth." John 18:37.
9. "We have a building of God, an house not made with hands, eternal in the heavens." 2 Cor. 5:1.
10. Ezekiel's vision of the river from the sanctuary. Ezek.

47:9.

11. "Remember the sabbath day, to keep it holy," etc. Ex. 20:8-11.

12. "Lendeth unto the Lord." Prov. 19:17.

13. Christ. Matt. 13:46.

14. "It is required in stewards, that a man be found faithful." 1 Cor. 4:2.

15. "Strive to enter in at the strait gate: for many, I say unto you, will seek to enter in, and shall not be able." Luke 13:24.

16. To the crackling of thorns under a pot. Eccl. 7:6.

17. Amos. Amos 8:11.

18. Ps. 107:23.

19. The men of Gibeon, because of their deceit. Josh. 9:3, 21.

20. Isaiah. Isa. 50:4.

21. "I and the Father are one." John 10:30.

22. "He that overcometh shall inherit all things; and I will be his God, and he shall be my son." Rev. 21:7.

23. "O how love I thy law! it is my meditation all the day." Ps. 119:97.

24. Samson. Judg. 16:30.

25. Philip, to the Ethiopian treasurer. Acts 8:27, 30.

SECTION 21

1. Elisha surrounded by the Syrian army. 2 Kings 6:16.

2. Haggai. Hag. 2:8.

3. Christ. Luke 13:32.

4. "Bear ye one another's burdens' and so fulfil the law of Christ." "For every man shall bear his own burden." Gal. 6:2, 5.

5. "All things whatsoever ye would that men should do to you, do ye even so to them." Matt. 7:12.
6. Job 11:7.
7. Elijah. 1 Kings 18:21.
8. The Israelites, just before the plague of fiery serpents. Numb. 21:5.
9. Paul. 1 Thess. 5:22.
10. Ps. 20:1-4.
11. "That we may obtain mercy, and find grace to help in time of need." Heb. 4:16.
12. Joseph, to Potifar's wife. Gen 39:9.
13. "Honor thy father and thy mother," etc. Ex. 20:12.
14. James. Jas. 5:11.
15. At Nazareth. Matt. 13:57.
16. Obadiah 4.
17. "Thy word is a lamp unto my feet, and a light unto my path." Ps. 119:105.
18. "They shall obtain gladness and joy; and sorrow and mourning shall flee away." Isa. 51:11.
19. Deut. 18:15.
20. Jehoshaphat. 2 Chron. 19:11.
21. "Wisdom is better than rubies; and all the things that may be desired are not to be compared to it." Prov. 8:11.
22. Pilate, of Christ. John 19:5.
23. Christ, to Saul. Acts 9:5.
24. "Who is so great a God as our God?" Ps. 77:13.
25. Jeremiah. Jer. 20:14.

SECTION 22

1. Hosea. Hos. 14:8.

2. Christ. John 10:37.
3. "But in lowliness of mind let each esteem other better than themselves." Phil. 2:3.
4. Abraham. Gen. 13:15.
5. "The fear of the Lord." Ps. 111:10.
6. Ezekiel. Ezek. 47:12.
7. "Whatsoever is more than these cometh of evil." Matt. 5:37.
8. Saul. Acts 9:6.
9. "Yet learned he obedience by the things which he suffered." Heb. 5:8.
10. "Woe unto them that join house to house, that lay field to field, till there be no place, that they may be placed alone in the midst of the earth!" Isa. 5:8.
11. Joshua. Josh. 10:12.
12. "Thou shalt not kill." Ex. 20:13.
13. "It giveth understanding unto the simple." Ps. 119:130.
14. Blind Bartimaeus. Mark 10:46, 47.
15. "Let him that is taught in the word communicate unto him that teacheth in all good things." Gal. 6:6.
16. "Say not thou, What is the cause that the former days were better than these?" Eccl. 7:10.
17. Naomi, to Ruth and Orpah. Ruth 1:8.
18. "All things were made by him, and without him was not anything made that was made." John 1:3.
19. The king of Sodom. Gen. 14:22, 23.
20. Balaam. Num. 23:8.
21. Joel 2:13.
22. "And shalt believe in thine heart that God hath raised him from the dead, thou shalt be saved." Rom. 10:9.
23. "For the Lord God Almighty and the Lamb are the temple of it." Rev. 21:22.

24. Joseph. Gen. 40:8.
25. John the Baptist, to Herod Antipas, concerning Herodias. Matt. 14:3, 4.

SECTION 23

1. Christ. Luke 11:41.
2. Paul. 1 Thess. 2:12.
3. Isa. 65:24.
4. Samuel. 1 Sam. 7:12.
5. David. Ps. 14:1.
6. Nebuchadnezzar. Dan. 4:3.
7. Peter and John. Acts 4:19, 20.
8. John. Rev. 11:15.
9. Christ, to the father of the demoniac son. Mark 9:23.
10. The Creator. Gen. 1:3.
11. Num. 6:24-26.
12. Christ. Matt. 12:30.
13. Paul. Eph. 5:2.
14. James. Jas 3:6.
15. Hos. 2:15.
16. Solomon. 1 Kings 3:7.
17. Joshua. Josh. 24:15.
18. The wisemen. Matt. 2:2.
19. Paul. Rom. 1:16.
20. Heb. 2:3.
21. Isa. 42:3.
22. Ps. 50:10.
23. Elisha, of Elijah. 2 Kings 2:12.
24. Job. Job 1:21.
25. To Ezekiel. Ezek. 3:17.

SECTION 24

1. Christ. John 8:32.
2. Paul. 1 Cor. 1:27.
3. The Lord through Moses concerning the passover. Ex. 12:14.
4. Job. Job 28:28.
5. Christ. Mark 16:15.
6. Song of Solomon 6:10.
7. Paul. Gal. 2:20.
8. David. Ps. 55:6.
9. Micah. Mic. 7:19.
10. Paul. 1 Tim. 1:15.
11. David, on the death of Saul and Jonathan. 2 Sam. 1:17, 19.
12. Ps. 97:10.
13. Eccl. 3:14.
14. Paul. 2 Cor. 1:20.
15. Prov. 15:3.
16. John the Baptist. Matt. 3:2.
17. Paul. Titus 1:15.
18. Moses to Joshua. Deut. 3:22.
19. Ps. 150:6.
20. Moses. Heb. 11:24, 27.
21. Lev. 10:10.
22. David, when his three warriors brought him water from the well of Bethlehem. 1 Chron. 11:19.
23. Peter. 2 Peter 1:20.
24. Ezra. Ezra 7:10.
25. Jude 24, 25.

SECTION 25

1. King Ahasuerus. Esth. 1:22.
2. Moses, of Asher. Deut. 33:24, 25.
3. Solomon. Prov. 1:7.
4. Christ. Matt. 12:34.
5. Paul, to the Thessalonians. 1 Thess. 4:11.
6. Satan, of Job. Job 2:4.
7. The Creator. Gen. 1:26.
8. The psalmist. Ps. 98:4.
9. Jeremiah, when called to be a prophet. Jer. 1:6.
10. The father of the demoniac child, to Christ. Mark 9:24.
11. Rev. 12:11.
12. Hosea. Hos. 4:6.
13. Habakkuk. Hab. 2:4. Quoted several times by Paul.
14. Peter, to Ananias, Acts. 5:3, 4.
15. Prov. 15:20.
16. Moses, to the Israelites, just before crossing the Red Sea. Ex. 14:13.
17. Moses. Deut. 4:24.
18. The angel Gabriel, to the Virgin Mary. Luke 1:28.
19. Paul. 2 Cor. 3:5.
20. Nehemiah. Neh. 4:6.
21. David. Ps. 55:22.
22. Christ. Luke 12:7.
23. Lev. 19:30.
24. Solomon. 1 Kings 8:22, 30.
25. John the Baptist. Matt. 3:8.

SECTION 26

1. John. Rev. 1:5, 6.
2. Ezekiel. Ezek. 8:12.
3. Christ. John 8:44.
4. David. Ps. 51:7.
5. David, of Jonathan. 2 Sam. 1:26.
6. Eccl. 4:12.
7. Paul, to the Corinthians. 1 Cor. 2:2.
8. David. Ps. 16:6.
9. God. Gen. 2:18.
10. Judg. 5:20.
11. Paul. Rom 2:1.
12. The children of Bethel, to Elisha. 2 Kings 2:23.
13. Isa. 43:2.
14. Nahum 1:7.
15. Paul. Eph. 5:14.
16. Samuel, to Saul. 1 Sam. 10:6.
17. Job. Job 31:17.
18. Song of Solomon 8:6.
19. Christ. John 8:51.
20. 1 Tim. 1:17.
21. Peter. 2 Pet. 2:9.
22. Heb. 12:1, 2.
23. Moses. Deut. 33:27.
24. Mordecai to Esther. Esth. 4:13, 14.
25. Peter and the other apostles. Acts 5:29.

SECTION 27

1. Christ, when left behind in the temple at the age of twelve. Luke 2:49.
2. Paul. 1 Cor. 4:20.
3. John. Rev. 21:23.
4. "Wine is a mocker, strong drink is raging: and whosoever is deceived thereby is not wise." Prov. 20:1.
5. The four lepers who discovered the departure of the Syrians. 2 Kings 7:9.
6. Christ, concerning the ass's colt. Mark 11:3.
7. "The wages of sin is death; but the gift of God is eternal life through Jesus Christ our Lord." Rom. 6:23.
8. James. Jas. 5:15.
9. "Some trust in chariots, and some in horses: but we will remember the name of the Lord our God." Ps. 20:7.
10. Samuel. 1 Sam. 12:17.
11. Job. Job 12:2.
12. Paul. 2 Cor. 5:6.
13. Pilate. John 18:38.
14. Zech. 3:8.
15. Paul. 2 Thess. 3:1.
16. After Elijah's sacrifice on Mt. Carmel. 1 Kings 18:39.
17. "My God, my God, why hast thou forsaken me?" Ps. 22:1.
18. "O Jerusalem, Jerusalem, . . . how often would I have gathered thy children together, as a hen doth gather her brood under her wings, and ye would not!" Luke 13:34.
19. "Godliness with contentment is great gain." 1 Tim. 6:6.

20. "Ye shall know them by their fruits. Do men gather grapes of thorns, or figs of thistles?" Matt. 7:16.
21. "Whosoever shall call upon the name of the Lord shall be saved." Rom. 10:13.
22. Christ. John 10:38.
23. See 1 Cor. 13.
24. Joab. 2 Sam. 10:12.
25. Rev. 21:27.

SECTION 28

1. "In the day of prosperity be joyful, but in the day of adversity consider: God also hath set the one over against the other, to the end that man should find nothing after him." Eccl. 7:14.
2. Balaam. Num. 24:17.
3. Job. Job. 13:15.
4. "And the life was the light of men." John 1:4.
5. Paul. 1 Cor. 14:40.
6. Ananias, concerning Saul. Acts 9:15.
7. Joel. Joel 2:28.
8. Ps. 79:13.
9. "Thou shalt not commit adultery." Ex. 20:14.
10. The seraphim in Isaiah's vision. Isa. 6:3.
11. The multitude, in Christ's triumphal entry. Mark 11:9.
12. "Leaveneth the whole lump." 1 Cor. 5:6.
13. Pilate, refusing to change the title on Christ's cross. John 19:22.
14. Isaiah, when called to be a prophet. Isa. 6:8.
15. To Abraham, in promising that Sarah should have a child in her old age. Gen. 18:14.

16. "Entreat me not to leave thee," etc. Ruth 1:16, 17.
17. Whosoever shall smite thee on thy right cheek, turn to him the other also." Matt. 5:39.
18. "Be not forgetful to entertain strangers: for thereby some have entertained angels unawares." Heb. 13:2.
19. "That which I do I allow not: for what I would, that do I not: but what I hate, that do I." Rom. 7:15.
20. "Whosoever exalteth himself shall be abased; and he that humbleth himself shall be exalted." Luke 14:11.
21. To Jonah, during the great storm. Jonah 1:6.
22. "The LORD's name is to be praised." Ps. 113:3.
23. "And into the patient waiting for Christ." 2 Thess. 3:5.
24. Of Lazarus. John 11:4.
25. "Divers weights, and divers measures, both of them are alike an abomination to the LORD." Prov. 20:10.

SECTION 29

1. "Even a child is known by his doings, whether his work be pure, and whether it be right." Prov. 20:11.
2. Christ. Matt. 7:20.
3. Peter. Acts 9:40.
4. Pharaoh's chief butler, remembering his promise to Joseph of two years before. Gen. 41:9.
5. Deut. 19:21.
6. Elisha's servant, after the sacrifce of Carmel. 1 Kings 18:44.
7. Christ. Matt. 14:16.
8. Christ. Rev. 3:19.
9. "This we commanded you, that if any would not work, neither should he eat." 2 Thess. 3:10.

10. Ps. 119:165.
11. "Thou shalt not steal." Ex. 20:15.
12. Hazael. 2 Kings 8:13.
13. "The Lord is my shepherd," etc.
14. Songs of Solomon 2:1.
15. Christ, in the parable of the marriage feast. Matt. 22:8.
16. Paul. Rom. 10:14.
17. Rev. 22:11.
18. Joshua. Josh. 23:10.
19. Isaiah. Isa. 52:7.
20. "And those that seek me early shall find me." Prov. 8:17.
21. Paul. 2 Cor. 5:7.
22. John the Baptist. Luke 3:7.
23. "For whatsoever a man soweth, that shall he also reap." Gal. 6:7.
24. Nathan. 2 Sam. 12:1-4.
25. Christ, from the cross to His mother, with reference to John. John 19:26.

SECTION 30

1. In Zechariah. Zech. 3:10.
2. Jonathan. 1 Sam. 14:6.
3. Jeremiah. Jer. 29:13.
4. "But every man also on the things of others." Phil. 2:4.
5. Christ. Mark 11:17.
6. Isa. 7:14.
7. King Jotham of Judah. 2 Chron. 27:6.
8. Paul. 1 Tim. 6:10.

9. "Thou shalt not bear false witness against thy neighbor." Ex. 20:16.
10. Job. Job 14:1.
11. "Leaving the principles of the doctrine of Christ." Heb. 6:1.
12. "The effectual fervent prayer of a righteous man availeth much." Jas. 5:16.
13. "Go out into the highways and hedges, and compel them to come in, that my house may be filled." Luke 14:23.
14. Nathan to David. 2 Sam. 12:7.
15. "And the fulness thereof; the world, and they that dwell therein." Ps. 24:1.
16. Jonah. Jonah 2:3.
17. Paul. 1 Cor. 5:7.
18. "Grace and truth came by Jesus Christ." John 1:17.
19. God. Deut. 2:3.
20. The king in Christ's parable of the marriage feast. Matt. 22:12.
21. Peter. Acts 10:15.
22. Joel 3:14.
23. Joseph. Gen. 41:16.
24. Samuel, to Saul. 1 Sam. 15:22.
25. Simon Peter. Luke 5:5.

SECTION 31

1. Joshua. Josh. 23:14.
2. "It is naught, it is naught, saith the buyer: but when he is gone his way, then he boasteth." Prov. 20:14.
3. Zechariah. Zech. 4:6.

4. "Whosoever shall compel thee to go a mile, go with him twain." Matt. 5:41.

5. Of Paul and Silas at Thessalonica. Acts 17:6.

6. Paul. Phil. 2:5.

7. Job. "All the days of my appointed time will I wait, till my change come." Job 14:14.

8. "Thou shalt not covet," etc. Ex. 20:17.

9. Jehu the son of Nimshi. 2 Kings 9:20.

10. "I will lift up mine eyes unto the hills." Ps. 121:1.

11. "Have seen a great light." Isa. 9:2.

12. The risen Lord, to Mary Magdalene. John 20:17.

13. Timothy. 1 Tim. 6:12.

14. "If any man hear my voice, and open the door, I will come in to him, and will sup with him, and he with me." Rev. 3:20.

15. Jeremiah. Jer. 31:3.

16. "But he that doeth the will of my Father which is in heaven." Matt. 7:21.

17. "He which converteth the sinner from the error of his way shall save a soul from death, and shall hide a multitude of sins." Jas. 5:20.

18. "They sold the righteous for silver, and the poor for a pair of shoes." Amos 2:6.

19. Abraham, when God proposed to destroy Sodom. Gen. 18:25.

20. Eccl. 7:29.

21. Christ, walking to the disciples on the sea. Matt. 14:27.

22. Paul. Rom. 7:24.

23. Peter. 1 Peter 1:8.

24. "He hath heard my voice and my supplications." Ps. 116:1.

25. Song of Solomon 2:4.

SECTION 32

1. "Believe that ye receive them, and ye shall have them." Mark 11:24.
2. "Faith cometh by hearing, and hearing by the word of God." Rom. 10:17.
3. "The Spirit and the bride say, Come. And let him that heareth say, Come. And let him that is athrist come. And whosoever will, let him take of the water of life freely." Rev. 22:17.
4. King Hezekiah, of Sennacherib. 2 Chron. 32:8.
5. "He that sinneth against me wrongeth his own soul: all they that hate me love death." Prov. 8:36.
6. Christ. Matt. 22:14.
7. Paul. 1 Cor. 15:3.
8. "After the power of an endless life." Heb. 7:16.
9. "He should have fed them also with the finest of the wheat: and with honey out of the rock should I have satisfied thee." Ps. 81:16.
10. John the Baptist. John 1:29.
11. Paul. 2 Cor. 5:14.
12. "The grace of our Lord Jesus Christ be with you all. Amen." Rev. 22:21.
13. "When thou shalt vow a vow unto the LORD thy God, thou shalt not slack to pay it." Deut. 23:21.
14. "Mercy and truth shall go before thy face." Ps. 89:14.
15. "Let us not be weary in well doing: for in due season we shall reap, if we faint not." Gal. 6:9.
16. To Martha, just before raising Lazarus. John 11:25.

17. "Buried with him in baptism." Col. 2:12.
18. "My soul longeth, ye, even fainteth for the courts of the LORD: my heart and my flesh crieth out for the living God." Ps. 84:1.
19. Paul. 2 Thess. 3:13.
20. Amos. Amos 3:3.
21. Heb. 13:4.
22. Lot. Gen. 19:20.
23. "If any man come to me, and hate not his father, and mother, and wife, and children, and brethren, and sisters, yea, and his own life also, he cannot be my disciple." Luke 14:26.
24. "There is therefore now no condemnation to them which are in Christ Jesus, who walk not after the flesh, but after the Spirit." Rom. 8:1.
25. "Give to him that asketh thee, and from him that would borrow of thee turn not thou away." Matt. 5:42.

SECTION 33

1. Pharaoh. Gen. 41:38.
2. Samuel, speaking to Saul. 1 Sam. 15:26.
3. "I will; be thou clean." Matt. 8:3.
4. Col. 2:21.
5. Paul. Rom. 11:29.
6. On meeting his disciples in the upper room after the resurrection. John 20:19.
7. "When the LORD shall bring again Zion." Isa. 52:8.
8. Moses, after the giving of the Ten Commandments. Ex. 20:20.

9. They shall walk, O LORD, in the light of thy countenance." Ps. 89:15.

10. Jonah. Jonah 3:4.

11. Peter, after the great haul of fishes. Luke 5:8.

12. "Let us do good unto all men, especially unto them who are of the household of faith." Gal. 6:10.

13. Job, to his three friends. Job 16:2.

14. Deut. 25:4.

15. "Unto us a child is born, unto us a son is given: and the government shall be upon his shoulder: and his name shall be called Wonderful, Counsellor, The mighty God, the everlasting Father, The Prince of Peace." Isa. 9:6.

16. "Render to Caesar the things that are Caesar's, and to God the things that are God's." Mark 12:17.

17. Peter, when worshipped in the house of Cornelius. Acts 10:26.

18. "That they be not high-minded, nor trust in uncertain riches," etc. 1 Tim. 6:17-19.

19. Christ to Peter, as he was sinking in the waves. Matt. 14:31.

20. Zechariah. Zech. 4:10.

21. After his exile and repentance. 2 Chron. 33:13.

22. "The LORD is thy shade upon thy right hand." Ps. 121:5.

23. Sarah, when Isaac was born. Gen. 21:6.

24. Jeremiah. Jer. 31:33.

25. "In the resurrection they neither marry, nor are given in marriage, but are as the angels of God in heaven." Matt. 22:30.